Jennifer
Needle in Her Arm

Healing from the Hell of My Daughter's Drug Addiction

by

Bonnie Kaye, M.Ed.

CCB Publishing
British Columbia, Canada

Jennifer Needle in Her Arm:
Healing from the Hell of My Daughter's Drug Addiction

ISBN-13: 978-1-77143-161-3
First Edition

Library and Archives Canada Cataloguing in Publication
Kaye, Bonnie, 1951-, author
Jennifer needle in her arm : healing from the hell of my daughter's drug addiction
/ by Bonnie Kaye. -- First edition.
Issued in print and electronic formats.
ISBN 978-1-77143-161-3 (pbk.).--ISBN 978-1-77143-162-0 (pdf)
Additional cataloguing data available from Library and Archives Canada

Cover artwork by Maureen Kavaney Tillman:
http://MaureenTillman.blogspot.com and
http://MaureenTillman.etsy.com and
http://maureen-tillman.fineartamerica.com

Publisher: CCB Publishing
British Columbia, Canada
www.ccbpublishing.com

This book is dedicated to three people:

- To **Lynne Abraham**, the former District Attorney of Philadelphia. Ms. Abraham taught me that a stranger can be a lifeline during your most desperate times. She was mine. I am forever grateful.

AND...

- To **Trisha Kinderman**, who never gave up on Jennifer long after everyone--including me--did. She was the best friend Jennifer ever had. While others washed their hands of Jennifer, Trisha never did. She is my constant reminder of the best of part of Jennifer.

I love you Trisha!

AND...

- To **Beverly Kelly** who gave me hope and comfort when there wasn't any to find. Beverly took care of Jennifer during her Fresh Start days when my heart was aching with despair.

Special Thanks

I would like to give special thanks to my friend Maureen Tillman who has designed the beautiful cover of my book. Maureen is an extremely talented artist and writer. You can view her artwork at

http://MaureenTillman.blogspot.com

and

http://MaureenTillman.etsy.com

and

http://maureen-tillman.fineartamerica.com

I would also like to thank my special friend Gail Bender Hersh who saved me the agony of typing up Jennifer's letters and poems by doing it for me. It is difficult just to read them, and I wasn't up to typing them.

Contents

DRUG DEATH, JENNIFER NEEDLE IN HER ARM

Introduction

It has been twelve years since the death of my daughter, Jennifer, who died at the young age of 22 in 2002. The loss of a child is the most horrific experience that any parent can face in life. It doesn't matter what the cause of death is--a loss is a loss. But when you lose a child to heroin, it is a double death because as a parent, you are dying a slow death with your child throughout the journey of his or her drug use, abuse, and final demise because you feel powerless to stop the ultimate disaster facing the child you love.

My daughter Jennifer's death was a double-edged sword for me, and I spent a long period of time grieving. I reacted the way that most good parents do whose children died from drugs by second guessing ourselves *for failing our children*. We keep questioning over and over and wondering what *we* did wrong--what *we* could have done differently--what signs did *we* miss--why were our children so unhappy that they had to turn to drugs to numb their pain? What pain could have been that overwhelming to reduce a beautiful child that we loved and cherished into nothing more than a gutter rat running through the sewer system of hell for a hit of drugs?

Eight months after Jennifer's death, I was introduced to another woman, Sue, whose daughter overdosed and died from heroin at the age of 16. She asked me to attend a local chapter meeting of a support group called Compassionate Friends, a nationwide organization that helps parents find support after the death of a child with others who have also experienced this devastating tragedy.

I first heard of the organization during the months following my daughter's death from a dear friend of mine, Chuck, whose own son had died as a young child. Chuck was actively involved in the Mississippi chapter of Compassionate Friends and strongly encouraged me to attend a local meeting. I really did not want to go--I wanted to mourn Jennifer on my own--but when Sue kept asking me to go with her, I agreed to do it.

Compassionate Friends had some extremely remarkable people who truly were compassionate to everyone at the meeting. Attendees were at all different stages of their grief; some had recent deaths they were just starting to mourn over while others had children who died over ten years before. They brought pictures, tee-shirts and buttons with their children's pictures to display, and candles to light. Each person went around the room and spoke about how his or her child died.

After attending the meeting, I realized that this was not the proper forum for me to grieve. Parents in the group had lost their children through all kinds of tragedies. They went around the room talking about car accidents by drunken drivers, drive-by shootings, and traditional diseases such as cancer or leukemia. I was the only person in the group of nearly 30 people who discussed the death of my child due to narcotics.

Although people were very kind, several of them were clear in their comments afterwards that they believed my daughter had a choice in her death while theirs didn't. I did not take it personally at that moment because I, too, waivered in my thinking when it came to "choice" and "drugs." During the three-and-a-half years that I spent navigating my daughter's very dark world called "*recovery*," I often believed the same thing--it was a "choice." She had a choice and made the wrong one.

Incidentally--this could have been my perception from one local chapter meeting of Compassionate Friends. I have recently seen the organization's itinerary for their current annual national meeting, and there are subgroups that directly address parents who lost their children to drugs. This may have changed because of the staggering number of deaths from drugs over the past decade creating more of an acceptance or a need for support from the group.

I would like to reiterate that the loss of every child is unique. There is no loss that is a better loss than another. I know that because less than three years later, I lost my 23-year-old son to a rare genetic disease he had been born with. But there are different emotional issues to deal with for each set of circumstances.

One of the common bonds that all parents with children of drug deaths face is the feeling of guilt, shame, and blame. You question yourself over and over what you could have done differently that would have changed the course of events. The "if onlys" play through your mind thousands of times. The sense of self-blame plays havoc on you for years to come.

Ironically, after that meeting at Compassionate Friends, two women came up to me and quietly thanked me for my story. They listened to me but "passed" on the opportunity to share the story of their children's deaths from drugs when it was their turn because they felt a sense of shame and being judged.

That's when I realized that support for parents of drug children needed more than just support--it needed some rebuilding of the long broken spirit that we all had in common in order for us to heal and grieve properly.

Support groups were not new to me. I had run several of them throughout the years for various causes, primarily as a counselor who specialized in working with women who unknowingly found themselves in marriages to gay/bisexual men which may sound unique, but it happens to over 4 million women in this country. I have been a pioneer in this field since 1984 after my own marriage failed for that reason and to date have worked with nearly 100,000 women helping them to put their lives back on track. Due to my personal tragedy of losing a daughter to drugs, I felt ready to start a support group for other parents who were suffering this specific loss which was different than other kinds of losses.

I started a local support group in my neighborhood of Northeast Philadelphia that met weekly for almost seven months. Then it was time for me to stop. I wasn't able to do my own healing because it was too soon after Jennifer's death. Telling my story each week for the new parents who joined us kept taking me back to a very painful place that I was trying to escape. Although my intentions were good, the timing was bad. I was unable to move forward myself. The women who remained found other sources of support to help them.

Selfishly, I was unable to resume this support group again in future years after I finally was able to grieve and come to terms with my daughter's death. Why? Because I did not feel like being dragged back into the drug environment which was a dark road filled with gruesome pain. I attended several vigils for children of drug deaths conducted by friends I made through the support group. This gave us a way to remember our children and inform the public of their humanity.

I remember the parents all carried crosses with their children's names on them. I had a Jewish star constructed with Jennifer's name and picture to show people that this disease goes across all boundaries. After attending these vigils for three years, I stopped going. I needed to put this behind me and really didn't want to talk about it anymore. I had learned much too much about a side of life that I never wanted to know about. It was a very evil side of life that had no light or hope. Also, at that time my son had just died, and I was much too hurt to hear about the hurt of others.

Throughout the past ten years, some troubled parents with drug children found their way to me through other people or the Internet, and I did my best to give them support and advice. However, I decided I wasn't up to doing it in a group or on a regular basis. I wasn't able to "detach" myself enough from the tragedy of my own losses and felt ineffective to take a leadership role in a support group.

With that being said, perhaps you are wondering why I'm writing this book. There are two reasons why.

1) I am writing about the journey I traveled with my daughter Jennifer during her drug addiction so that other parents going through this battle will understand that they are not alone in their struggle. The feelings of guilt, shame, blame, and failure that many of us feel are isolating and destructive. I hope that when you read this story, it will address your own feelings of guilt and self-doubt so that you can move ahead in your life.

2) Jennifer left me a number of writings that she had wanted to share with others. I am hoping that maybe--just maybe--it will change the course of events for someone on the edge of drug addiction. Some of her words are chilling, but they were written to be heard and to help.

This story is not only for the parents whose children have died from drugs but also for those parents whose children are still walking through the "valley of the shadow of drug death" awaiting their turns to get that last phone call as they continue down the "one-way street to that final moment." This isn't a book of false hope or illusions--just the story from one mother about one daughter to help you understand what is still not--or may never be--understandable to any of us.

CHANGING WHERE THE BOOK BEGINS

After finishing this story, I decided to start with an article I wrote the year following my daughter's death. Why? Isn't it unusual to start at the end before the beginning?

I realized that this book may be painful for parents to read. My main hope in writing this book is for you, the parent or family member, to have some closure. You may never get to the message on healing and forgiving yourself if you have to stumble through the story and stop because of the hurt it may bring back to you.

After you read this article, hopefully, the story will be easier for you to read. After this article was written, the State of New Jersey asked me if they could post it on their website where it stayed for nearly a decade. I hope it will bring you some comfort and validation along your journey.

GAMES PARENTS WHO LOSE CHILDREN TO DRUGS PLAY THE "IF ONLY" AND THE "BLAME" GAMES

By Bonnie Kaye, M.Ed.

I have met too many parents who assume that the reason for their child's death from drugs is due to something *they, the parents,* did wrong. For most of us who have had time to work through this problem over a longer period, it gets easier for us to understand that we are not responsible for our child's drug habit and ultimate death. But if you go back to the early days following the death of your child and the initial horror you felt, you'll be able to remember those strong feelings of self-doubt, second guessing, and taking responsibility.

When I reflect on my own inner thoughts of guilt after my daughter Jennifer's death, I remember feeling a great sense of responsibility. I used to play a game that most of us fall prey to. I call it the "If Only Game." It goes like this. "If only I would have been a better mother...if only I spent more time with my daughter...if only I would have gotten my daughter more help...if only I wasn't so demanding...if only I was more supportive...if only I was stricter...if only, if only, if only...then maybe my daughter would never have turned to drugs and ended up dead."

I then moved into another phase, which I call "The Blame Game." A few weeks after the death of my daughter, I looked to place blame everywhere I could. First I blamed my ex-husband, her father, for not being more supportive during her growing up years and recovery journey. Then I blamed her friends who knew that she was doing drugs but never told me. I blamed the police who were able to spend time giving tickets to people at parking meters, but couldn't spend the same time finding the drug dealers selling heroin to my daughter. I blamed the District Attorney for not prosecuting these criminals in a more punitive way. I wasn't able to accept her explanations of how as soon as the dealers were locked up, new ones were on the street. I blamed everyone and everything that I could logically or illogically come up with because I wanted someone to take the blame for this horrible tragedy. Most of all, I blamed myself. See the "If Only" game above.

The reason why we are so quick to fall into the traps of these games is because the death of a child from drugs makes us feel such a strong sense of inadequacy as parents. We bring our children into the world with hopes and aspirations for their happiness and success. When they are young children, we can fix all of their problems. We are their protectors. They depend on us and look to us for safety. When something is broken, they count on us to fix it--and we do. If they had a problem in school, we'd go marching into the principal's office assuming that the school was the problem--not our child. Many of us fixed our children's problems even when we knew they were the ones at fault. This is what happens with *unconditional* love.

After being able to keep our children out of harm's way for so many years while they were growing up, we found ourselves totally ineffective and helpless to save them as they turned to drugs. Most of us blame ourselves for not recognizing the seriousness of the problem. We ask ourselves a hundred times, "Why didn't we see that our child was using drugs?" We wonder, "How stupid could we have been not to see the signs?" The truth is that most of our children were clever and knew how to hide what they were doing. *And most of us were naive and had no understanding of drugs.* Some of us suspected that *maybe* our kids tried marijuana or some pills like almost all kids do today. None of us believed that our children would turn into hardcore addicts who would destroy their lives and the lives around them.

There are those of us who feel guilty because we threw our children out of our homes when we couldn't deal with their addiction anymore. Others feel guilty because they didn't practice "tough love" and allowed their children to stay at home, enabling their addiction. There is no right or wrong way to deal with addiction. There are no guarantees or best practices advice. We are on our own, trying to figure a way to end the nightmare.

We all went to doctors, hospitals, and organizations looking for help. We learned the politically correct lingo from groups and organizations that work with addiction. "Your child won't recover until he/she hits *ROCK BOTTOM*." We didn't understand what that terminology means. When do you reach *rock bottom*? My daughter overdosed on three different occasions as they pounded her body to bring back a heartbeat. While I stood there hysterically crying in the hospital, I was so sure that she had hit ROCK BOTTOM. Sadly, that wasn't *rock bottom* enough--obviously. It seemed that selling her body for a hit of heroin was as low as she could go, but she still didn't hit *rock bottom.* Having men beat you up and steal your money from prostituting was the next step down, but that still wasn't *rock bottom.* Getting locked up for prostitution seemed one step even below that lowest step. But even that wasn't *rock bottom*. I still have no idea what *rock bottom* is. In Jennifer's case, *rock bottom* was death.

You do the best you can as a parent. You try any expert advice to save him or her, but when everything fails, you often make that cut away from your child because you can no longer put your family in jeopardy. An addict not only destroys his/her life, but the lives of the family members as well. You are a hostage in your own home because if you leave it, something of value will be missing when you return.

I loved my daughter dearly. I sympathized with her for three of the three-and-a-half years of her addiction before I cut her off. Over those three years, I moved her from detox, to rehab, and into numerous recovery programs including halfway houses and clean houses. I re-mortgaged my home and invested the money into programs that convinced me that they had the answers to “cure” her. Maybe they did, but my daughter wasn’t listening. She knew the 12 steps to recovery upside down, inside out, and led meetings galore. She was a natural leader. She had a period of time when she managed a recovery house and threw other users out of the house when they came in high. When she was good she was very, very good. But when she was bad she was horrid. And that’s an understatement.

In Jennifer’s good moments when she was clean, she was a loving, endearing, and happy daughter filled with jokes and laughter. During her relapse back into addiction, she became a monster whom I didn’t recognize. She would be angry--full of accusations when she couldn’t get her daily fix. She’d be cursing at me, her brother, and her father, while blaming us for all of her unhappiness. Then when she’d get her dose of poison or during lucid moments in recovery, she’d be remorseful, trying to convince us that it wasn’t she who was talking--rather it was the heroin that took over her body making her talk that way. It was like living in the movie “The Exorcist” when Linda Blair’s body would spew filthy words to everyone around her because she was *possessed.*

I was always feeling sorry for my daughter. Part of my reason was because she was giving up the best years of her life. This was before I realized she was just giving *up her life period*. She spent at least half of that three-and-a-half year period going through recovery programs. Every time I would visit her, I walked away feeling an incredible sense of sadness. While her friends were spending this time in college dorms, she was sitting in recovery houses and programs with up to 30 women, sleeping 3 – 6 in a room. There was no privacy. You were in full view even when you were in the bathroom. The curriculum consisted of 12-step exercises and books about your higher power. The lecturers were not visiting professors, but rather recovering addicts recounting their years of addiction and how they lived in gutters with rats just to get a hit. The classmates were not bright, optimistic young adults trying to learn the about their future careers. Rather they were people with dual or multiple diagnoses--bi polar, depression, anxiety and drugs all rolled up into one.

Some of them were mothers who abandoned their own homes and their children in return for a high. They landed in a crack house because the lure of drugs was much stronger than the lure of family. There were ones who were even worse--they sold their children for a high. They were mixed between the young and the middle aged. Some of the women were mandated by courts at the end of their prison sentences to stay there; others were novices like my daughter when she entered her first program, filled with hope that there would be some kind of “magical cure.”

There were no cures. There were just some clean times. And each time I packed Jennifer’s bags for a new rehab, all I could hope for was that the clean time would become longer and the relapsing would be shorter. There were no false hopes given to me by the professionals who cared for my daughter in these programs. If anything, I was assured that her chance of failure was high. She was young. Young people rarely recovered. If only she could live it out, maybe she would burn herself out.

Some people told me that the best thing was to get Jennifer arrested. I was horrified at that thought. I couldn't see my daughter in a cage 4 x 6 feet locked up like a criminal. She was an addict--not a criminal. Even when she robbed me of all of my worldly possessions three years into her addiction, I couldn't do it. I knew that the heroin had made Jennifer into a criminal, but I still couldn't do it. Would it have saved her life? I'll never know. But she would have been emotionally dead in a prison--mentally broken down from living in a cage. And, then again, if prison were the answer, so many addicts who get out of prison wouldn't return to drugs. And they do.

Tough love experts talk about "enabling." I was blamed for supporting my daughter's habit because all of the financial support I gave her was used to support her addiction. And yet, five months before she died, I cut her free from support so I would stop aiding her habit. I spoke to her, but I wouldn't see her or give her money. Well, there was one time I saw her. That's when Jennifer slit her wrists a few days before her 22nd birthday. She called for help, and we went to help her once again. It had been three months since I last saw her after starting "tough love." It wasn't a pretty sight. She had lost a lot of weight, joking about how the only way she was able to beat her chronic weight problem was when she was using heroin. I didn't find it funny. I looked at my daughter with track marks all over her arms in between the cuts. There were oozing ulcers on her body from the constant use of needles in her arms.

I don't think she was really trying to end her life at that time. The wounds were too superficial. But I took it as a cry for help. After dropping her off at the local mental health hospital in order to get her into a detox, once again she went through the torture of detoxing on methadone. Several days later on her birthday, I had a load of her clean laundry delivered to her detox program with a birthday card and twenty-five dollars. I was still very angry, but I couldn't allow her to feel abandoned on her special day. Six days later when she was to be released after promising me daily that she would enter a new program, she fled and went back to the streets. She left me a message on the phone of how sorry she was once again to disappoint me. And I cried in horror that I was back to "no hope" once again.

After Jennifer's return to the streets, she'd call me approximately every seven to ten days. The time was fairly consistent--2:00 a.m. in the morning. Addicts rarely have a sense of time when they are high. She would call me at her lowest moments, like after being robbed at gunpoint by a trick. She'd be crying on the phone.

"Help me Mommy."

"Okay, Jennifer, are you ready to go into a program? If you are, I'll pick you up now."

"I'm almost ready Mommy. I'll call you in the morning. I love you."

The call never came. This went on five or six times until I got my final call on April 14, 2002 at 2:00 a.m. The call was from the hospital telling me to come to the hospital. When I got there, they wanted me to claim my daughter. She was dead.

Obviously, tough love didn't save her. Enabling her didn't save her. She was doomed. Heroin had taken its hold on my daughter and wiped out all thoughts of rational thinking. She had no chance.

Allow me to share some reasons why guilt overtook me during my first year. I know I'm not the only parent who said or thought terrible things in anger and frustration over those years of her drug use. Jennifer's addiction kept me very busy running, going, and working. I stood with her for the first three years--body and soul. She was the best-dressed girl in rehab. I made sure of that. I made sure she had whatever she needed each time she started over. I didn't want her to have even lower self-esteem than she already had. I gladly paid for programs, detox centers, doctors, hospitals, halfway houses, and apartments every time she wanted help. I was willing to pay for her to be anywhere--except living with me.

I always wanted to help her addiction, but I didn't want to live with it. On the days that she had to stay with me because she was waiting for an opening in a program, I felt trapped not being able to leave my house in fear of what I would find when I walked in--or rather, what I wouldn't find. There were days that I hated my daughter. There were moments when I wished she had never been born. And there were still other moments when I wished she vanished because the pain she was causing all of us was so great.

When we lose our children to drugs, all of those angry feelings surface to the top of our memories as we grieve our loss. All of the angry words that were said resonate loud and clear. Those are the memories that cloud all of the years of love we gave our children. We dig back into the early years of their lives and mysteriously remember the occasional negative words or punishments, trying to put our finger on what we did that pushed our children over the edge. I find that parents either think they were too hard on their children or not hard enough. We feel that we failed our children, not that they failed us. That wouldn't make sense. Our children failed us? *Nope, we were the failures.* It doesn't matter if you have other wonderful children who grew up in the same home with the same parenting. We must have done something different with our drug children. After all, they turned to drugs.

We consciously or subconsciously feel this need to make the death of our children OUR responsibility. Why? Why do we feel the need to blame ourselves for something that wasn't within our control? Simple. We were good parents. Somehow, we lose sight of this when our child dies. We look for all of the things we did wrong instead of remembering all of the things we did right. We let our imagination run rampant looking for the "bad" we did rather than remembering the love we gave and good things we have done. This is human nature. Selective memory takes over. We drag out memories from when our kids were young and we yelled at them...we disciplined them...we punished them...we criticized them. We are looking to pin the blame on ourselves. Somehow, we drag up these isolated incidents and *voila!* We now understand why our children had to destroy their lives with drugs. It makes sense, doesn't it? NO. It makes no sense at all.

We allow our hearts to overtake our brain when a child dies. After all, in the scheme of life, parents are supposed to die before their children, not vice-versa. If a child gets killed in a car accident or drive-by shooting, it's a tragedy. But when a child dies from a drug addiction, it's a tragedy with blame--so we think. Why were our children in such pain that they had to stick needles in their arms, legs, and necks to numb their senses? Who caused that pain? We, the parents? I don't think so--anymore. But I sure did early on.

Drugs are rampant in our society. It's just a fact. They are accessible and easy to find. They are on our corners, in our schools, and on the playgrounds. They are even more accessible than alcohol was to us when we were growing up. Our kids are looking for excitement and adventure. Some of them find it through drugs. That's just the way it is. Most kids will experiment. And those of them that are predisposed to addiction will make it a way of life--and ultimately, death.

There's no such thing as a *perfect parent.* But I guarantee you that none of us encouraged our children to feel better or solve their problems by popping pills, shooting needles into their veins, or snorting powder up their nose. We gave them the best advice and guidance we could. And in almost all cases, we were loving, caring, and protective parents who wanted the best for our children.

Playing the "If Only Game" and "The Blame Game" is a very natural part of self-questioning that all of us go through in the day, weeks, and months following the death of our children. The problem is that some of us get stuck there, sometimes for years. This is a dangerous game if played for too long because it indicates that you have not been able to put things into perspective and move into the stage of acceptance. Your emotions have overtaken your ability to rationalize things clearly. It also stops you from moving ahead and trying to rebuild your life. Prolonged questioning of your parenting failures serves no purpose at all. If you failed at saving your child from drugs, it's because you were in a no-win situation. Drugs set you up for failure, not for success. *Success was not an option with drugs.*

I have come to terms with my daughter's death by viewing it as a disease much like cancer. When I would go to Narcotics Anonymous meetings with my daughter, I used to hear the word "disease" used quite often. I refused to buy into it. Drugs were a choice--not a disease. I don't feel that way anymore. *Drugs are a disease*. They seep through the body and poison it, just like cancer. Maybe our children have clean periods of time, which I equate with remission during cancer. But eventually, the cancer is back, rearing its destruction all over again. Heroin is a death sentence. Other drugs like crack are just a prolonged death sentence.

When my daughter first told me about her addiction, I was very naïve.

She said, "Mom, the recovery from heroin is one in a hundred."

I wasn't discouraged, but rather encouraged.

I said, "Jennifer, that's great.

She looked at me strangely and said, "Mom, why would you say that is great?"

When I said the following words, I said them with total sincerity, determination, and hope.

"It's great because there is a one out of a hundred chance of recovery. It's not totally impossible. You'll be the one out of a hundred who recovers."

Of course, when I said those words I didn't understand heroin. I had no clue about how it would take over my daughter's body physically, and the lure would overtake any attempt or efforts of not wanting to take it. I have now accepted that it was a pull much too strong for my daughter to fight. I am not angry with her. She was a victim of a terrible tragedy.

Now, shortly after a year-and-a-half of her death, I have stopped blaming Jennifer for her drug habit. And I have also stopped blaming myself. I loved her, I cherished her, and I gave my all to help her. And I know as a fact that she loved me. I try to stay away from the painful dark places of thinking what her final weeks and days were like. That is a space that hurts too much. I put up a protective shield in my mind that screams "STOP!" when I start going there. It serves no purpose whatsoever. I have stopped punishing myself. Throughout the first year of Jennifer's passing, I tried to make sense out of her death, but there was no sense to be made out of it. I have stopped questioning, "Why?" and just accepted it.

Time is a strong healer. My heart will never totally heal. There will always be a space cut out that can never mend. But as time passes, I am able to look at the happy memories instead of dwelling on the horrors of the end of her life. I have allowed my thinking side to overtake my emotional side, or at least to catch up to it. Life will never be the same, but it has become better. I can now look at parents who are enjoying their children without having resentment for what I don't have. I try to remember the good times we did have, and that gives me comfort. What I find the most comfort in is knowing that my daughter is no longer in pain or in harm's way. She really is in peace. Her disease is not torturing her anymore, and that is the most I can hope for.

You can write to Bonnie Kaye at
Bonkaye@aol.com
July, 2003

CHAPTER ONE

WHO IS JENNIFER'S MOTHER?

In order to understand my life with Jennifer, I would like to tell you a little about me, her mother. I was born in 1951, the oldest of five children. My first decade was one of 1950's suburban innocence. As a child, I sat with my parents in my comfortable home watching all of the black and white sitcoms of the day that reflected the perfect family life. Those shows included *Father Knows Best*, *The Donna Reed Show*, and *Ozzie and Harriet*.

We really were naive in those days. I remember at the age of 11-years-old playing with my school friend Ross who was visiting. We walked outside to play hopscotch, and we saw that someone had written the word "FUCK" in chalk on the ground. I had heard the word before somewhere and knew it was a bad word, but I had no idea what it meant. When Ross told me, I looked at him with horror. He swore that was how people made children, but I insisted that my parents would never do such a disgusting thing. Fifty years later, that incident is still ingrained in my head. Those were the days of innocence I grew up with.

The days of illusion faded quickly and became disillusion when my parents divorced in 1965 and I was age 15. Divorce was unique in the suburbs during the 1960's, and families felt stigmatized by it when people whispered behind your back and stopped socializing with you. My parents were very progressive, but their marriage was a disaster. The divorce certainly left its imprint on my mother and my siblings.

In 1968, at the age of 17, I was a very mixed up--or rather screwed up--teenager. My father owned a number of bakeries, and having worked in them from the age of nine, I never really made a connection to a child's world. I wanted to be with adults because I felt more comfortable there than with the snobby suburban kids who looked down on me. I suffered from a condition that millions of people suffer from--"low self-esteem." Back then, I didn't understand what that term meant or how to change it. I was doing self-destructive activities centered around being promiscuous which made me feel "wanted." I was never one of the "pretty girls" who could attract a popular guy based on my looks. I was always chunky trying to fit into those "chubby" sized racks in the clothes store. I lacked grace and coordination that the popular girls had. However, by the age of 15, I became popular because I would give the boyfriends of the cheerleaders something they weren't willing to give--namely sex.

I had just turned 17 at the start of my senior year in high school in 1968 when I met a man who was 11 years my senior. He was hanging out with people I knew in our apartment building. Harry was attractive, and more importantly, he was enamored with me. I was flattered that a mature man wanted to date me, and I eagerly accepted his invitation to start seeing him. It seemed strange to me that he was always taking cough medicine, and sometimes he would ask me to pick it up for him. Back in those days, cough medicine with codeine didn't need a prescription, but it did need a signature when you bought it. I was too naive to understand that this was a drug. I used to ask him why his cold was never getting better showing sincerely worriment. Actually, this was the least of Harry's addictions. Harry was a heroin addict. Heroin was a drug I heard about, but I never had actually met anyone who was doing it.

Five months after meeting Harry, I became pregnant. It was intentional because I was miserable living at home with my mother and looking for a way out. I believed if I was pregnant, she would let me move out of the house to get married--but I was wrong. My mother refused to allow me to leave when I finally built up the courage to say those words "I'm pregnant" to her. She made it clear to me that I was going to have an abortion because there was no way that I could be a responsible mother in my situation.

I may have been rebellious, but for some reason, I accepted my mother's decision most likely because I knew she was right. It was the best decision she ever made for me. How could I have been a mother? What could I have offered a child? I was going with a man who was a drug addict living with his elderly grandparents and had no job or way to support us. I was 17-years-old and in the midst of dropping out of school. Back then, you were forced to leave high school if you were pregnant. An abortion in 1968 was very difficult because it had to be approved by three different psychiatrists. When I finally received approval, I stayed in the hospital for three days following the procedure. How different abortion has become over the years!

One vivid memory that stayed with me from that hospitalization was what my mother said to me as I left the hospital. I saw a woman and her husband carrying out their new baby wrapped in a pink blanket. They looked so happy holding the baby. My mother saw me glance over to them and sensing a moment of sadness, she said to me, "Someday you will have a baby the right way. You'll have a husband who can be a father to your child. You'll have a career where you make enough money to give a child what she needs. That's why you'll be ready to be a mother." Those words were hard to swallow, but I knew my mother was right.

The following week after the abortion, my mother sent me to California to stay with my father. She was no longer able to handle me because I was out of control. I didn't blame her. I really was on my own page, and she had my three younger sisters there to raise. She believed through my poor choices that I would be a bad influence on them.

California in 1968 was culture shock for me. Drugs were starting to be more known in my hometown of Philadelphia by that time, but it was confined primarily to marijuana--and I had never tried it. Even though Harry was addicted to heroin, I never saw him do it nor did I have a clue to how people did it. I didn't even know he was on heroin until I called him to say goodbye when I was leaving town. He then told me he was going into a drug program to get better from his addiction. By that point, I knew I really didn't want Harry anymore because it was obvious that he had no future other than getting high.

Incidentally, Harry died from drugs two years later shortly after I returned to Philadelphia from California. He had left the strict drug program, Synanon, twice and never returned. He had just started a new drug replacement, methadone, which wasn't regulated correctly in 1970. Patients would receive a week's supply and of course, take it in a day or two to stay high. On the weekend of Harry's death, it was a holiday. He was given a two week supply of methadone and was told to take the proper amount daily. Well you know the story--give me a bag of

Hershey kisses, and they will be gone in the first day or two. The same happened here, and Harry's body couldn't handle the extra doses of methadone.

When I arrived in California in 1968, drugs were rampant. My younger brother, Lance, had moved out there the year before because he didn't like living with my mother and his four sisters in a cramped two-bedroom apartment where we moved after my parents divorced. He was14-years-old when I joined him there, and he had told me that he was into taking drugs as well as dealing drugs.

Lance encouraged me to try drugs, but I was only willing to try smoking marijuana. I enjoyed the euphoria I felt when I joined in smoking it at the parties we went to, but that was as far as I wanted to go. At that point, Lance was taking LSD and "tripping" two or three times a week. He would tell me stories of how beautiful colors and pictures would appear in front of him. He really wanted me to try it with him, but I was very scared. I didn't know much about drugs, but I did hear terrible stories about people who took LSD and had bad trips. I even knew someone who had jumped out a window and died from his hallucinations. Why would I want to take that chance?

Lance convinced me that LSD came in different varieties, and he guaranteed me that the kind he used didn't create those kinds of reactions. After all, he had already "tripped" over 100 times and never had a problem. One night, I gave in and agreed to do it with him. It was the most frightening experience I ever had. All kinds of images kept attacking my mind, and I had no control over them. The first thing that jumped out at me a half-hour after taking the pill was a "dancing" leprechaun which was part of an advertisement display for a liquor store my brother worked for. I knew the journey--or "trip"--had begun. I remember going swimming that night in a pool, crossing over Santa Monica Boulevard with no regard for the oncoming traffic, and not being able to close my eyes to sleep it off because images kept jumping in my brain. I hated it. I hated being out of control and not knowing what was going to appear next. It was like walking through a haunted house and having scary figures jump out at me for hours. Even now, over 40 years later, I can clearly recall getting into the house, and when I turned on the television, watching a commercial for a local pizza place. On the ad was a promotion for a mushroom pizza, and the mushrooms started dancing on top of the pizza.

When it came to drugs, I was scared. I didn't see the point of feeling "zonked out" and "tuned out" like so many other people were doing. Pot or hash was fine at a party, but that was the only time I was looking to smoke it--and that was as high as I wanted to be. A half of a joint was more than enough to knock me out. When I was offered other forms of drugs like Quaaludes or black beauties, I just said "NO."

I had my own addiction that I was fighting my entire life--namely a food addiction. I have been a food addict since early childhood. In spite of over 50 years of constant dieting, diet pills, the eating disorder of bulimia for over two decades, and a failed gastric bypass that nearly took my life, I still am an obese adult. It was understanding my food addiction that gave me the misdirected feelings of compassion first for my brother and then for my daughter. My reasoning always was that if I couldn't stay away from a Hershey bar, how could I expect them to stay away from narcotics which has a much stronger hold on people? Yes, I was sympathetic based on my own weakness to sugar.

When Jennifer was seven years old, my brother moved from California to live in Philadelphia. He had burned all of his bridges out there with his drug habit. At that point, he had nowhere to live because our father had kicked him out of his house for the last time. Lance had broken his leg and was on crutches, but my father said he could no longer have him stay in his house because his addiction had become too overwhelming. With nowhere to go, my mother paid for his plane ticket and invited him to move in with her. Wearing crutches when he arrived at the airport, he bemoaned how my father kicked him out of his house during his worst time of need. In all fairness, my father gave Lance countless chances to change over 17 years, but he refused. He wanted to stay stoned.

My mother had good and loving intentions when she extended an invitation for him to live with her. She really didn't understand how addicted my brother was to drugs. She felt she could "control" it even though my father warned her on several occasions. In other words, she was clueless. My brother had never discussed his addiction with her, but I knew from my father that he was doing heavy duty drugs. Much like I believed later with my own daughter, my mother believed that love and understanding would chase away my brother's drug addiction. We were not drug educated. We were both totally uneducated. I had been exposed to drugs during my two years in California--and I was still naive. I wasn't part of that world, and I didn't have much contact with people who were drug users other than the one incident with Harry when I was 17.

After a week of Lance living with my mother, she called and asked me to take my brother to live in my home. She was not equipped to handle him in her house falling down stoned, falling asleep with cigarettes in his mouth, and putting burn marks in her sheets and blankets. She loved my brother, but she was scared to death to have him in the house when she was working.

Living with my good natured, drug-addicted brother was a real challenge for me. On one hand, we were very close. He could make me laugh like no one else could. He had a big heart after he took care of his own needs, but finding drugs on a daily basis was always a challenge and always his first priority. That came first--finding the drugs. My brother robbed everyone's medicine cabinet. He had previously been using heroin in California, but then switched over to narcotic pill combination called "sets." When mixed together, they gave him that same heroin high. My brother lived at dentists' offices with made up "tooth pain" in order to get these legal prescriptions that got him illegally zonked out. It was a daily job finding drugs to sustain his habit.

By Lance's second year of living with me, he enrolled in a methadone clinic. Each day he would drive 25 minutes to get his daily dose to help level out his need for other narcotics. At least he didn't seem as desperate to rob everyone's house for drugs anymore. Of course, what I didn't know for a long time was that my brother was able to supplement his methadone with other pills that he bought right outside "the clinic." Yes, drug dealers know where to find drug addicts--at the methadone clinics. No doubt there are some addicts who are trying to the right thing and just maintain themselves on daily methadone; however, there are many addicts who use the methadone to get their early dose of drugs and the readily available other drugs for later in the day.

I loved my brother even though living with him in my house scared me. I had to set up fire alarms in every room because when I would go down to the basement where he lived, he would be zonked out with cigarette filters still in his mouth with the ashes falling on his face. The bed, his clothes, the blankets, and sheets all had cigarette burns in them. I was so afraid a fire would start--but it never did.

My brother worked to pay for his habit. He was a mechanic and made a living working out of my garage fixing cars. He also had a weekend job delivering pizzas for the quick cash he needed for his drug habit. He was cute and had a great personality, so it wasn't unusual for him to make between $200 - $300 dollars for 3 nights' work. He was also invited to party with a number of the people he delivered pizza to, so he felt it was the perfect job for him--quick cash and high times.

Some people are just not meant to die in fire. This was my brother. He escaped dying in a car accident even though he was stoned most of the time while he was driving. He also managed never to burn himself to death even though he fell asleep with the cigarette dangling from his lips while dropping burnt ashes all over his face. I had smoke alarms in every room of my house then and equipment to put out fires on every floor.

On a side note, his addiction was more than a physical one--it was also a mental one. There was one time during this period when he stopped using all drugs except the methadone. He looked like a new person--and he acted like one as well. It was the best I had ever seen him. He was looking clean as far as his appearance. He was acting "straight" instead of zonked out. He said he was fine as far as the addiction because the methadone was enough for him to sustain himself on. Every day was a miracle, and my whole family gave him so much positive feedback and support during that span. Then as suddenly as it started, it ended six weeks later. Things were back to "abnormal."

When I questioned Lance why he felt the need to go back to the drugs, he told me that he didn't "fit in" to the straight world. He didn't know how to act or how to interact. If he wasn't using, he didn't have his drug friends. He had all of this extra time on his hands and found himself bored. He was like a stranger in a strange land and couldn't adjust. After 19 years of being in a different world since the age of 13, he was really lost in this world. I thought that was an amazing insight from someone who only knew drugs his whole life.

When my brother died in my house during the Christmas week of 1986, I felt devastated and guilty. Devastated because my brother was my best friend and guilty because I had a fight with him the day he died. I was angry at him for something irresponsible he had done. I remember talking to a friend of mine on the phone and saying how angry I was with him while making sure I spoke loud enough for him to hear it. Then I went out with my two children to K-mart to buy gifts for the holiday season. I felt so guilty about saying bad things about my brother that I ended up buying a few extra presents for him out of guilt.

When I would go shopping with the kids, I always told Lance to be ready to help me come in with the packages. On that night, I drove to the back of the house to get him to come out and help me with the packages. I knocked on the back door, but there was no answer. I heard loud music playing, so I thought maybe he didn't hear me. I then drove around to the front of the house and brought the children inside. Once I had them in there, I went to the door that separated my floor from the basement. I started knocking on the door and calling his name, but there was no response.

An eerie feeling came to my chest as I turned the door handle to start my walk downstairs. I kept calling Lance's name as I walked down the basement stairs one step at a time. When I reached the bottom step, I could see him sitting in a chair with his back to me. I kept yelling at him, but there was no response, He was hunched over peacefully in the chair. I started screaming and screaming and shaking him, but I realized that he would never move on his own again because he was dead. In shock, I called the police. The rest of the details are blurry now since it is over 25 years ago. The worst thing I had to do was call my mother to tell her that her only son (we had four girls) was dead.

I believe in some crazy way that during that first year following my brother's death that my mother held me responsible for not being able to save him. In retrospect, she was most likely playing the "Blame Game" that I wrote about earlier. She withdrew from me in her grief. My mother never knew how to really mourn this death other than to drink. Drinking numbed her sorrow because she wasn't willing to deal with it in a way that was healthy. I realize after experiencing this myself that her self-imposed guilt for not saving my brother threw her into this state of mind.

In the months following this tragedy, I also suffered with tremendous guilt. I wondered if Lance had taken more drugs that night because he heard me saying something mean about him. I questioned why I didn't insist that he get more help to beat his addiction. I know I had tried so many times, but he was an honest addict. He loved to be high, and it had been the only life he knew since the age of 13. He didn't want to change, and so he died the same way he lived--high.

His autopsy showed that Lance didn't die from an overdose, but rather from a toxic build up of narcotics over the years. This gave me some relief because I realized it wasn't my harsh words that led him to take extra drugs.

In the aftermath of Lance's death, I spent many days listening to people with different opinions of how I should have handled the situation. Some said I was right to protect my brother and let him stay with me; others said I could have saved him if I practiced "tough love." Sadly, I wasn't much of a "tough love" type of person at that point. I didn't see any alternatives. I knew if I would kick Lance out of my house, he would die on the streets. He wasn't capable of making it independently. He wasn't looking to change, and although I tried to encourage him daily, he took no interest in recovering from addiction.

I was in college at the time of Lance's death. He was 33-years-old and two-and- a-half years younger than me. One of the courses offered at the university was about addictions focusing primarily on drug and alcohol addiction. I spoke to the professor hoping for some guidance and looking for some solace. He told me that I did the best I could do. No one could tell me a right or wrong way to do things. I had to follow my gut instincts in order to live with my decisions. It was somewhat comforting, but I replayed that scenario in my head over and over again. On one hand, if I threw Lance out of my house, he could die on the streets. Would I want that on my conscience? This same no-win choice would haunt me 15 years later with my own daughter. I could never believe the nightmare that was waiting for her in the unforeseen future.

Ironically, both of my children were part of the anti-drug campaign while they were elementary school. Jennifer at the age of seven was able to see the devastating effects of Lance's death on our family. When she was in fourth grade, she came to me feeling very proud that she had joined an organization in school named D.A.R.E. This organization went into schools to talk to kids about the effects of drugs as a preventative measure. Jennifer was so proud when she brought home her certificate for participating in the program.

I saved that certificate with pride only to realize it didn't work in the future years of Jennifer's teenage turbulent times. I was so confident that drugs would never be an issue with my children seeing how much pain our family suffered over Lance's death.

There is an important lesson I learned from Lance's death that I would like to share with you. Many of us feel the "shame" of losing a child to drugs. I grew up in a middle-class Jewish family where drugs were never talked about or discussed. As I mentioned earlier, when my brother died, my mother was so heartbroken that she couldn't even grieve. In all of the years after Lance's death when people asked her how her son died, she would say, "Heart attack." *She never could say "drugs."*

My grandmother, my mother's mother, was the pillar of wisdom in our family. After Lance's death, she would always say that we have nothing to be embarrassed about. After all, the Kennedy's lost a son to drugs several years earlier. She was referring to David Kennedy, son of Robert and Ethel Kennedy. My grandmother said if the Kennedy's were not exempt, what made us think that we would be. Everyone and anyone could fall victims to this. It did provide some comfort to me, but not to my mother who could never deal with Lance's death in a healthy way.

Jennifer Needle in Her Arm

CHAPTER TWO

WHO WAS JENNIFER?

Jennifer was born seven weeks premature in 1980. My pregnancy was relatively normal; I had some early bleeding, but it turned out she was kicking on the lining of my uterus causing me to bleed. I was so terrified at the thought of losing her. Jennifer wanted out by the middle of the seventh month, and that began the pattern of her having her own way throughout her life. I don't know if that was a coincidence or if it was predetermined like so many other things were before she was born.

Back in those days, women who delivered through a caesarian birth stayed in the hospital for eight or nine days following the surgery. Since Jennifer was so premature, she was unable to eat on her own. In those first few days of being in terrible pain from surgery and frustration from not being able to feed her an ounce of milk, I don't believe that "bonding" connection that people talked about happened between us. Jennifer had to be "force fed" after the first two days, so that exasperating job was taken out of my trembling hands.

I was 30-years-old when my daughter was born. I was excited about becoming a mother, but I was also scared. I desperately wanted a baby, but I didn't have a clue on how to be a mother. I was also apprehensive because I knew I was bringing a child into a marriage that was already problematic. I was hoping that the miracle of birth would be the miracle to stabilize my marriage which was shaky at best. Jennifer's dad desperately wanted a child, so I hoped that the birth of our daughter would focus us more on being a closer family unit.

Jennifer was a beautiful little baby. She had sparse platinum strands that later turned into long and flowing blonde hair and big blue eyes. I remember in her early months when she would be sleeping in her crib, I would watch her movements feeling mesmerized. If she would start to frown or distort her face, I was alarmed thinking that she was having a bad dream. I would grab her little hand and softly rub it with loving words. I remember always thinking that I felt so helpless when I couldn't protect my little baby from a bad dream. I loved her so much, and I just wanted her to always feel loved and protected.

She was such a smart baby who knew how to recognize the 26 letters of the alphabet by the time she passed her first birthday. We spent lots of quality time together during her years from infancy through kindergarten. After her father and I split up when she was only two-and-a-half years old, I was home most days. I went to college in the evening, so we had some excellent bonding time together with her baby brother by our side.

In her early years, Jennifer was very difficult for me to handle. She gave new meaning to the term "terrible two's." She was defiant when I didn't want her to do something that she wanted to do yelling loudly the word "NO." I was worried that the turmoil of my marriage and the subsequent departure of her father may have left her feeling confused or frustrated. At that point, I went to a child psychologist who told me that I had to learn how to be "consistent." Consistent? What did that mean? She explained I couldn't give in to her no matter how temperamental she behaved.

The therapist was in her late 20's and didn't have any children, and I explained to her that text books don't necessarily have the answers to the day-to-day life problems that mothers encounter. After four sessions, I quit going to the sessions feeling more "consistently" frustrated. I wanted the therapist to interact with Jennifer, but she claimed that was not how therapists worked with children--it was through the parents.

The terrible two's became the treacherous three's, but by the time Jennifer turned four, she was a wonderful, loving child who had mysteriously turned from a devil to an angel. She was so sweet and funny--I now believed what people said about those early years. The terrible two's and three's would pass--and they did! Jennifer was so pleasant in nursery school that she won special awards for congeniality.

Jennifer was amazing in school in her elementary school years. She was a straight A student, and in first grade, she scored perfect marks in her city-wide testing. I really believed the future was hers which is why I worked so hard to get through college during that time. I wanted to be able to get a sustaining job with a respectable income to make sure she had the best of everything in life.

It's funny how some kids just seem to get away from you as they are growing older. Jennifer was always quite independent. I believed she was a leader. She was always smart--sometimes too smart for her own good. At 13, I noticed she was hanging around some girls from the neighborhood who were reputed to be smoking pot. I confronted her several times about it only to be told that it was a lie. She reassured me that she would not hang around pot smokers. In later years during her recovery, she admitted she was doing pot and a whole lot more with those friends, but at the time, I believed my daughter when she told me "No."

I knew that she was having issues with self-esteem from the time she graduated elementary school. She was an overweight teenager, and my heart went out to her because nearly my whole life was spent as an overweight person from my pre-teenage years throughout my adulthood. I tried to build her self-esteem on a daily basis praising her by telling her how beautiful and smart she was, but anyone who knows the truth about low-self esteem also knows that it comes from how you feel about yourself internally--not the messages your mother gives you.

When Jennifer started high school at the age of 15, I sensed she was having "problems." It was difficult for me to pinpoint exactly what these problems were, but in all honesty, I never suspected drugs. One day at the age of 16, she came home to me all excited about a new group that she had joined. When I questioned her further, she said it was a girl's group to protect girls--similar to the political activism I was involved in during the 1970's. I thought it sounded a little strange because Jennifer never seemed to express any interests in political events. Eventually she revealed the name of the group to me--The Crypts.

I wasn't tuned into groups that were violent at that time. The most violence I exposed my children to was the World Wrestling Federation matches that they loved to watch with their friends cheering for the Million Dollar Man or Hulk Hogan. When my daughter said the name of "Crypts," I thought it was a nickname for group that was into vampires like my kids watched on television. My first moment of distress came several weeks later when I found a big letter "C" branded into Jennifer's arm which she kept well hidden from me by wearing long-sleeved shirts. I was sick when I saw it. She explained that all of the girls in the group did it to "initiate" each other into the group. They took a wire hanger, formed it into the letter "C," heated it over the stove, and then pressed it against their skin.

Now I was starting to panic. I told Jennifer that she was no longer allowed to be part of a group that would practice violence. She explained that she was trying to get out of the group, but it wasn't quite that easy. It would take time--you couldn't just "quit." I kept pressing her on the timeline fearing she would get in serious trouble, but she said that she was "handling it." I actually felt so desperate that I went to the Gang Control Unit of the police department to talk to them about my fears. Although they were sympathetic, they didn't take the group very seriously. They explained that they were aware of the group of girls from the area that were involved in the activity, but they were just acting like "wanna-be's" wearing red or blue bandanas on their heads and making threats or doing juvenile types of crimes like painting graffiti or bullying. Their time needed to be spent on the real gangs around the city that were using real weapons for shooting and killing people. They told me if I ever found out anything to let them know, and they would follow up on it. I felt somewhat discouraged when it came to help from the officials, but I understood that my wayward daughter was not the priority of their unit.

Over the next few weeks, I saw Jennifer was spending less time with the group. I learned several years later when she decided to leave, she had to be "beat out" by the other members. I couldn't understand why a relatively well educated group of girls had to live life on the edge doing such dangerous things. I was so grateful when Jennifer's gang activities ended, and I thought I could finally have peace of mind.

Several months after leaving the Crypts gang, I realized for the first time that Jennifer was exhibiting signs of sociopathic behavior. An incident started one night during the summer when she came home at 9:00 p.m. Her curfew was 11:00 p.m., and that was always a battle because she kept pushing to stay out later during the summer. On this particular night, I couldn't understand why she was home so early. When I asked her, she replied that it was chilly outside, and she didn't have a jacket. I knew there was something wrong because it was 80 degrees outside. She started acting very edgy, looking nervous and scared.

Finally, after asking her a half-dozen times what was wrong, she told me that she had to leave home. My heart sunk, and I started to panic. I told her that there wasn't anything that bad that we couldn't fix. I told her no matter what it was, I would be by her side and begged her not to think about running away.

I finally got her version of what happened. Jennifer explained that she was hanging out with some of her friends that evening. They were minding their own business when they passed another group of kids who knew them from school. One of the girls, Dawn, started calling her names and pushing started. Jennifer claimed that Dawn fell down, and when she did, she cut her mouth. Jennifer "swore" that is how the accident happened, but she thought the girl would say that Jennifer pushed her down to the ground and that was why she was bleeding. Jennifer explained the girl was wearing braces which cut into her gums which caused the blood.

I was still a believer in my daughter's lies at that time. I held her as she cried, promising her that I would stand by her no matter what. I was hoping that nothing would happen, but Jennifer was so scared the police would turn up at our door that night. I had her sleep in my bed to make sure she knew she wasn't alone. She slept very restlessly even though I held her just like she was my baby again.

Several days after this incident, we received a summons to go to juvenile court for a hearing. Dawn was pressing charges against Jennifer. I spoke to an attorney who looked into it for us, and he said not to worry. He checked with the court and it was not likely that any action would be taken against Jennifer other than probation or community service as long as she appeared calm and rational.

The day of the hearing is one that would always stay in my mind. This was the day of realization about Jennifer's "other personality" that totally blindsided me. I remember we were sitting in a large courtroom. The other girl, Dawn, was there with her parents. We had rehearsed a dozen times what Jennifer would say--she would admit the argument got out of hand and that she didn't recognize her own strength. She would apologize profusely and offer to repay any financial fees for damages that had resulted from the incident.

Jennifer went up before the judge and explained her side of the story. She acted quite apologetic and remorseful. The judge dismissed the case with a stern warning stating he better never see her back there again. He took into consideration that she was doing well in school and had a loving mother to support her emotionally. We never told her father for fear he would lose control and physically hurt her. I knew for sure that the emotional abuse would have been overwhelming when he lashed out against her. Although her father loved her dearly, his level of patience was very limited.

As we left the courtroom, the moment of reality struck me. I felt so happy that we could put this behind us. I was so grateful that nothing more severe happened. We went out of the courtroom, and when we were walking down the hall, I saw Jennifer smiling with a smirk-like smile. I was puzzled.

"Why are you smiling?" I asked her in a very annoyed tone.

Her response was, "I beat it!"

She showed absolutely nothing but contempt for the proceedings. I explained how lucky she was to have a judge let her go when she could have been in serious trouble including jail time. I was a wreck--she wasn't. That's when I realized the problem was major. For the first time, I realized Jennifer had sociopathic traits.

You may ask me why would I ever label my daughter with this painful psychological term that means someone who lacks empathy and has the inability to know right from wrong. Simple. She exhibited so many of the tendencies that I just refused to see or chose to make excuses for. After all, who wants to admit that the little blonde haired, blue-eyed girl that I brought life to could hurt innocent people? This was my big girl who wrapped her arms around me every time she saw me and kissed me saying, "I love you mommy."

In hindsight, I have no doubt that this behavior of pain was exhibited to others on a regular basis. Three years after Jennifer's death, I met a young lady who told me how Jennifer had destroyed her life. She told me that throughout high school, she'd have to run home each day and hide because Jennifer would stalk her, threaten her and push her down. Jennifer was a big girl who was extremely strong. In high school she went by the name Jen Dog. I don't think it was given to her as a sweet name--but rather because she was like a pit bull.

This poor girl said she hid for three years in high school from Jennifer and her girlfriends who bullied her into a nervous breakdown forcing her to be hospitalized. She said she wasn't upset at all when she heard that Jennifer died but rather relieved. She felt that she could now walk freely in her neighborhood. That's how much damage Jennifer had done to her. I felt so mortified when she told me this story. I knew Jennifer had many issues, but bullying weaker people was inexcusable. Who was this stranger in my midst? I felt then that I never really knew her at all.

By the time Jennifer turned 16 ½, she came to me one day and told me that she wanted to live with her father. This happened after one of our increasingly frequent arguments that was particularly rough. Jennifer's personality was similar to her father's when she was angry--loud and yelling. My son and I had opposite personalities and tried to avoid conflict whenever possible. From the time Jennifer was in her mid-teens, I was used to yelling back at her when I was pushed into it, but this time she had been so disrespectful that I pinned her against the wall. That was one of the great things about Jennifer--she always respected me and loved me enough not to push back. She was extremely physically strong and could have easily hurt me, but she never did.

At that point, I told her father that he really needed to talk to her about her behavior because I didn't have control over her. There were constant confrontations between us with her pushing the limits and creating more stress than I was able to handle. I had the challenges of caring for my chronically ill son, Jason, who had frequent hospitalizations for a rare immune deficiency disease that took his life three years after Jennifer passed away. I was working a full-time job and a part-time job to pay the bills. Coming home to a volatile daughter treating me with disrespect and breaking the rules took me back to the unhappy days of dealing with my ex-husband who shouted me down to shut me up throughout our marriage and our after-marriage years.

Whenever Jennifer and I would have a bad confrontation, she would call her father to complain about me. After one particularly bad fight, she called her dad to ask if she could stay at his house overnight. I drove her there relieved that I would get a break. That night, he lured her to move in with him by offering her a better deal than I did. I wouldn't let her stay in the house alone with her friends while I was working because I would find beer bottles and cigarette butts in my basement. Of course Jennifer always denied her involvement, but I explained to her that it doesn't matter if you are innocent of guilty--you are judged by the company you keep. She was compromising my values and disobeying my rules by allowing this to happen in my home. Although she proclaimed innocence, I was starting to see a pattern--she was the one that was guilty and dragging the others along. As I mentioned, I was working two jobs at that point, so it was important to have peace of mind while I was away from home. I never quite had it.

When Jennifer told me that she decided to move in with her dad, I felt a sense of relief. I loved my daughter, but I also wasn't prepared for her erratic behavior that erupted daily when she didn't get her way. I believed her father would be able to handle her much better since they both had strong personalities. Did I suspect the erratic behavior was due to drugs? No way. A few times when I saw Jennifer with blurry looking red eyes, I would ask her, "Jen, are you smoking pot?" After all, she was a teenager, and it wouldn't shock me. But when she would get so angry at me and shout, "Why do you keep asking me that? You know I have bad allergies," I felt a sense of relief that all was well with the world. Of course, I believed her.

As a side note, many years later when Jennifer was in recovery, she was in one of her "honesty" modes. She told me that during her high school years, she had used LSD over 500 times, nearly died from angel dust, and once she moved in with her dad, she was using the popular drug at the time Ecstasy which had a touch of heroin in it.

When Jennifer moved in with her dad, I spoke to her daily and saw her three or four times a week when we would hang out together having dinner or shopping for her clothes or other feminine needs. She was in eleventh grade in school when she moved in with her dad. It was a very big adjustment because she wasn't old enough to remember living with him because our marriage ended when she was only two-and-a-half-years old. She had spent time with him on occasional weekends and yearly vacation trips, but that wasn't the same as living with him.

In as much as both she and her father had similar personalities and traits, there was often a lot of loud fighting going on between them. They both had temperaments that clashed. Jennifer had asked me several times if she could come home, but I explained that she made a choice and she needed to stick with it. My life with her brother had become so much calmer than when she lived with us acting angry so often.

Sometimes I felt guilty about feeling relieved that she went to live with her dad. After all, I was her mother. Raising Jennifer had been so challenging since she reached adolescence. I tried to understand her and why she acted as she did, but I never quite reached the real inner parts of her. Once again, I reflected back to my own teenage years and how I was always doing misdirected things. They difference between my daughter and me was that the things I did were self-destructive. The things she was doing were destroying others first and then herself.

I don't think my parents ever knew me or understood me either. I'm not sure if I even knew myself. Maybe that's why I had as much empathy for Jennifer as I did. I only hoped that she would make better choices than I had at her age. In thinking back, maybe this was also the sign of drugs, but I had no clue.

Jennifer graduated high school in 1998 because her father gave her no choice. He refused to allow her to drop out because she likely would have done that if she had a choice. He spent many days going in to speak to the principal about her behavior, but somehow, he made her stay in school and achieve good grades. At her graduation in 1998, I was so proud when she won a scholarship to our local college. I felt moving in with her father had been the best solution because I felt sure if she lived with me, she would have been a high school dropout with no future.

Even though Jennifer and her dad often exploded, there was no doubt in my mind that he loved her and wanted the best for her. Her dad was just as naive as I was when it came to drugs. I remember one day while Jennifer was in 12th grade, he called me to his house in a terrible panic. He was having a fit because he found little plastic bags in Jennifer's room--the kind used for drugs or so we thought. Amazingly, we were still not really familiar with what "bags" used for drugs looked like. I stayed with her dad until Jennifer came home. He wanted me there when he confronted her. She looked scared when she walked in and saw both of us sitting there--a scene that she didn't see very often.

Her father told her to go down to her room. There he showed her the little plastic bags that he found hidden in her drawer and asked her why they were there. Jennifer blew it off saying, "Dad, why are you asking me this? You know I don't have anything to do with drugs."

She explained that her best friend had been arrested for fighting, and she asked Jennifer to hold on to the plastic bags while she was away in lock-up. Jennifer didn't even look in the paper bag they were in--she just went on blind faith that she was putting something away for her friend. She was just as surprised as we were when we showed her those little plastic bags.

Stupid? Yes. Relieved? Very. Did we believe her? Sort of. Remember, we wanted to believe her, and like other drug addicts, she was an awesome liar. Between the words of denial of the addict and the relief and belief of the family, it's a combination headed for disaster. And disaster was impending just around the corner for us.

When Jennifer graduated high school in 1998, she decided that she didn't want to go to college right away. She wanted to work for a year and gain some financial independence. I understood where she was coming from; after all, I didn't even graduate high school. I didn't obtain my GED until I was 26, and I didn't start college until I was 31. I also had that need to be on my own and living my life, and so once again, I projected my life into Jennifer's choices feeling sad but understanding.

By the end of the summer, a job finally came for Jennifer as a bank teller thanks to a friend of her dad's who was a branch manager. She was hired as a roving teller for a large bank chain filling in when people were out for vacation or illness. After a two-week intensive training session, Jennifer was working as an official teller by October 1998. I was so proud of her getting dressed up for work every day--which was certainly not her style--and going from bank to bank. Her father had bought her a car, so she was able to go around the city to the eight different locations in the district.

As soon as Jennifer started working, she informed us that she was ready to move out of her father's house and into an apartment with two of her friends. The apartment was only eight blocks from my house, and I was happy that she was staying in the area so I could see her. It was a two-bedroom apartment, and the utilities were included. She explained if the three of them split expenses, they would only have to each pay $300 a month. Jennifer was taking home $350 a week from the bank, so it sounded like it would work out financially.

I told Jennifer that I would help her buy things for her new apartment like new sheets, towels, plates, food, and some other necessities for her apartment. Her dad bought her some furniture, so she was set to go. Once again, I projected my need to live on my own from the day I turned 18, so I understood how my daughter was feeling. I wished her the best of luck, and she knew I would help however I could. The girls living with her were high school friends, so it sounded like it would work out.

It didn't take long until the fighting between the roommates began. At the end of the first month, one of the three roommates moved out. Jennifer told us not to worry because another friend was moving it. It appeared to be like musical friends--one would leave, another would come. I thought it seemed strange, but Jennifer assured me that the girls who were leaving were moving to different areas...joining the military.... going to college...lost their jobs and money...or some other plausible excuse.

In early January of 1999, I noticed something different going on with my daughter. She always was out or sleeping when I called her apartment. We only spoke once or twice a week during the first two weeks of the month. She needed food claiming that her money ran out on expenses she hadn't anticipated like car insurance and utilities. I bought her several bags of groceries, but when I went to deliver them, her roommate came to the car and said that Jennifer was sleeping, so she would bring them up to her and save me a trip.

A mother knows when something isn't right. She may not know what is wrong--but she does know something isn't right. I called Jennifer and left her several messages saying I wanted to see her. After two or three days of no response, I personalized it and stated, "You don't have enough time to see your mother? Why are you suddenly too busy to see me?"

She finally called me back after a week of harassing threats and told me, "I'm coming by to see you, Mom."

I will never forget the day in January--January 9-- when she came to visit me to drop her news. When she gave me her customary hugs and kisses, we sat down, and she apologized for not being in touch with me for the week. This is how the conversation went.

"Ma, I've been really sick for the past eight days. That's why I haven't called you."

"Jennifer, if you're sick you always call me. I'm always happy to take you to the doctor and get you whatever medicine you need. In fact, I just took you to the doctor two weeks ago when you were having horrible stomach pains."

"Ma, I was a different kind of sick this time, and you couldn't help me. It was just too horrible."

My heart started sinking thinking something terrible like a car accident happened leaving her injured and in such terrible pain she couldn't talk. I grabbed her (lightly as to not hurt her) and said, "Jennifer, tell me what happened? Did you have an accident?"

"No ma, the car is fine." I breathed a sigh of relief.

"So what is it that could be so bad?

"Ma, you won't understand or believe it. But I'm going to tell you. The reason I was so sick last week was because I was withdrawing from drugs."

My first thought: She WAS smoking pot after all!

She then said, "And the drug I was withdrawing from was heroin."

Now, I am sure that most other people would have gasped and clutched their chest, but not me. I was sitting there feeling relieved.

"Jennifer, that's great. I'm really proud of you. I feel terrible that you felt the need to try it, but I'm so glad you were able to get yourself off of it."

"Ma, I don't think you understand. I said HEROIN."

"Jennifer, I heard what you said. But you just told me that you spent a week going through hell to get it out of your system. Are you using it now?"

"No Ma, I'm not using it. I just withdrew from it."

"Okay, Jennifer, I'm proud of you--that's good news."

Jennifer looked at me puzzled.

"Ma, I don't think you understand what I just told you."

"Jennifer--I did understand what you just told me. You *tried* heroin, and you *withdrew* from it. I'm very proud of you for that."

Jennifer stood up in front of me and said, "Ma, I don't think you really understand. Only ONE in a hundred heroin users ever stops using it."

In all earnestness I replied, "That's great Jen! I'm glad to hear that."

"Ma, why in the world are you glad to hear that?"

My reply must have sounded very ridiculous to her, but I had no clue at that point just how ridiculous it sounded to my daughter--the heroin addict.

"Jen, you said that one in a hundred people recover. That's good news because you're going to be that one in a hundred. I will make sure of that. We will do this together and the problem will be over for you."

The sad thing is *I really meant it--and worse--I believed it.* Yes, I was naive. Yes, I had no idea about the enemy that entered my child's body at the age of 18 and decided to destroy her life. I was looking at my 18-year-old daughter and thinking to myself, "There is no way in hell that she can't overcome this at 18. She is going to be the one in a hundred to beat this problem."

I would live to choke on those words over the next three-and-a-half years during Jennifer's spiraling journey to hell.

Jennifer Needle in Her Arm

CHAPTER THREE

LIVING THE HELL

The following day, the first thing I had Jennifer do was quit her job at the bank. This was after she revealed to me later that previous night that since she started working there, she had stolen over $5,000. She had missed work the week before during her heroin withdrawal telling her supervisor that she had a bad case of the flu, so they were holding her job for her. I had her call and thank them but tell them she was resigning to go to school. I was amazed that in the four months she worked as a roving teller, she was able to pull this off; however, as I mentioned earlier, Jennifer was very smart. I learned later from the woman that helped her find the job that Jennifer was on shaky grounds there--not for the stealing which they never mentioned but due to her nodding off at her teller station which they referred to as "sleeping."

After having Jennifer quit the job, her father and I decided we would carry her expenses until she could find another job. We thought that since she had "detoxed" from heroin, her problem was behind her. We were in close daily contact with her making sure that she was okay. Of course, we were both clueless. We were still believing her lies telling us how well she was doing. Three weeks later, her father called me in a terrible panic telling me that Jennifer had overdosed and was taken to a local hospital. He was away on a trip, but one of Jennifer's roommates had his number and called him.

I ran to the hospital and was there within ten minutes, but the security guards wouldn't let me into the emergency room where Jen was being revived. I was a total wreck, crying and trying to push the guard away. Finally, I was allowed to go into the room. It seemed that each minute was an hour, and I was so, so frightened as my heart was pounding through my chest. You can only imagine a mother's fear of losing her child in an instant. When Jennifer was revived, she told me that she tried her best not to do drugs, but she weakened. She tried it one more time and overdosed because her system had been off of it for a few weeks.

After this, her father said we had to put her away in a program to help drug addicted people. He told her that she had to leave her apartment immediately and move back in with me. He didn't trust her alone, and I didn't disagree. Leaving her on her own led to her overdose. The problem was I didn't want her living with me because I wasn't home all day, and I couldn't trust her to be alone at my house. I took off from my job for the next few days and did some desperate research into housing alternatives. I went through the phone book and called the organizations people referred me to outside the Philadelphia area where there were "recovery" programs. Sadly, there were no beds available in these at all or in the near future. That meant I didn't have many choices. I would be happy for any facility that would take her quickly because programs would not take someone unless they weren't using at the time of entering.

One of the half-way houses that was filled told me about a place named Fresh Start located in a section of North Philadelphia called Kensington--a neighborhood that was known to be a big place for drug addicts both using drugs and in recovery from them. I felt hesitant about taking Jennifer into a neighborhood where drugs were so abundant, but the philosophy in recovery was that it didn't matter where someone was recovering because there would be temptation wherever they went after they were released. I guess it sounded somewhat logical to a desperate mother who needed to find a place for her vulnerable daughter.

Jennifer seemed happy to go with me to visit the facility. Maybe she was looking for some miracle as well. The staff there was very warm and welcoming. I remember walking up the steps to the building, holding her hand tightly as I did when I was taking her to nursery school at three-years-old, ringing the bell, and waiting with apprehension for someone to open the door. We were ushered into the main office to meet the director, Kitty, and the assistant director, Bev. Bev would become a true friend to this worried mother throughout the days and years ahead.

We walked through the facility and saw that it was spotless. There was a kitchen that the women shared to prepare their meals. There was a meeting room on the second floor, and bedrooms on the second and third floor. What struck me most were the bathroom stalls without doors. There were three sets of bunk beds in each room, and Jennifer would be assigned to a bed if she decided to go there. Any fears either of us had were calmed by the kindness of the staff and residents we met. Jen and I agreed she would be comfortable if accepted and made the commitment to go the next day after packing her belongings and finishing some admittance paperwork--a routine that would be repeated over and over again over the next three years.

I took Jennifer shopping that day and bought her everything I could think of that she would need including new sneakers, sweat suits, pajamas, and a jacket. I felt so, so terrible that my daughter was going to a "rehab." I thought if she had to be there, at least she would be the best dressed girl there. The next day after breakfast, I brought her to her new home where she would remain for the next four to six months in "recovery." If she did well during that time, she would be promoted to the next step up which was the building next door called The Work House. There she would be given more privileges and be allowed to go to work or to school.

We walked into the foyer of the building with her suitcase. I was told that Jennifer would be on "blackout" for the first seven days meaning there would be no phone privileges. Visits would have to also wait for two weeks. I hugged her goodbye in the lobby holding her so tight because that was as far as I was allowed to go. I told her, "I love you, Jennifer--I'll come as soon as I can." A young woman guided her to the upstairs while I burst out crying. Lovely Beverly was there hugging me and promising me that she would personally look after Jennifer so I shouldn't worry. I would never forget her kindness. My relationship with Bev would continue many years after Jennifer's death because I would never forget when someone extended any kindness to me or my children.

Fresh Start allowed family visits once a week on Sunday afternoons. I was so excited about visiting Jennifer on my first visiting day. I told her I would cook her favorite meal and bring it to her. She loved steak, and I made sure to by the best cut for her so she could enjoy the meal. When I arrived, there were big hugs and kisses. She seemed to be doing well--at least she looked good. She didn't love her kitchen clean-up duty, but as the new person on the block, she had to do some of the more unpleasant chores. At least I felt she was out of danger and away from drugs. She was one of the youngest there, so she had a bunch of "older sisters and aunts" trying to look out for her.

I was feeling optimistic. It was a feeling that I would delude myself with a dozen times or more over the next three years each time Jennifer fell down, went through detox, rehab, and recovery--only to relapse. Her first relapse came after less than two months at Fresh Start. I received a phone call from one of the administrators there that Jennifer had left. Left? Left to where? I panicked. Where could she be? My heart started palpitating as all kinds of horrible thoughts attack my brain.

I started calling around to Jennifer's friends hoping someone would know something about where she was. One of her friends called me the next day to tell me that Jennifer was okay trying to allay my worst fears. She had stayed at her house that night with her "girlfriend." I panicked--now Jennifer escaped with another participant. I worried it was someone who would go down that road of destruction with her. Her friend said, "No, I mean her girlfriend."

It didn't sound quite right to me the way she was saying "girlfriend," so I asked her what she meant exactly. She was somewhat taken aback when I pressed the issue further not knowing who this "girl" was. Once again, I was totally blindsided when she revealed the next part of our conversation."

"You know Jen is gay, right?"

"No, I didn't have any idea about that."

"Oh my God--I'm sorry I told you that. I thought you knew."

Now I was feeling somewhat numb. This was one more obstacle added to Jennifer's life that she was going to have to deal with.

A Lesbian. How could I have a daughter who was gay and NOT know it? How could I have a daughter who was a drug addict and NOT know it? It was getting worse by the minute. How could I raise a daughter from birth until almost adulthood and not know that she was interested in girls instead of boys?

Did this come as a total surprise? Well, yes and no. Yes, because I was clueless, and no, because Jennifer's father was gay. I was a counselor for women married to gay men and had worked with thousands of them at that point. I know that my chances of having a gay child was at least 10% higher than other people because of genetics. As someone who has now (as of the time of publishing this book) spent over 30 years studying this and worked with nearly 100,000 people who have passed through my support network, I am convinced this is true. I don't engage in arguments about homosexuality as a "choice." Heroin was a choice. Sexuality is not a choice--nor is it a preference. It's who you are as a person. I totally get that and hold to my beliefs.

Although Jennifer's dad was gay, it was far more difficult for him to accept Jennifer than for me. He went ballistic. It was a reaction I didn't expect from him. If anything, I was hoping for understanding. He blamed everything surrounding the circumstances:

"She's drug gay."

"She's heavy so boys reject her."

And when that didn't work:

"It's your fault."

At the end of the book, I have republished the article I wrote for my monthly newsletter *Bonnie*

Kaye's Straight Talk after Jennifer's death. In there, you will see how difficult it was for her father to accept Jennifer's homosexuality. There was never a time when he made her feel accepted as gay, but this *was not* the cause of her drug addiction.

When I asked Jennifer why she didn't tell me about being gay, she said she was afraid she would hurt me too much knowing how it had hurt me so much with her dad. I felt bad when she told me that because I had always brought her up in a very accepting environment towards homosexuality because I knew people didn't choose it--nor should they be judged because of it. I always wanted my children to feel secure in the love of both of their parents. I also know how children are composed of both parents--not just one--so it was important to feel good about both of the people they came from.

After much begging and pleading, Fresh Start was willing to give Jennifer another chance to come back there even though she went "AWOL." They counted her good time in prior to the AWOL as far as getting to the Work House. Eventually, she moved up to the next step for people who were able to have more freedom and work. A few weeks later, Jennifer told me that she wanted to move out of there. It was "too crowded... too hot...too restrictive..." for her. She found a place that was a "safe house" where she could have her own small room with a bed. She told me even though it was a small space, at least it would be hers. I wasn't happy about this change, but I was afraid if she was getting that antsy that if I said no, she would go to a house that wasn't "safe."

Okay, once again, I was naive. I knew the program was crowded. In the midst of the hot summers in Philadelphia the building was steamy. Jennifer did have breathing problems, so I didn't want her asthma to kick in even worse. I went along with her and gave her the money she needed to get started. She told me as soon as she was situated, she would invite me over to visit.

Her new room was on top of a restaurant in the Kensington section of the city. Jennifer said she was comfortable there because that is where her "recovery" support was located. She had her meetings and her "clean" friends who were helping her at this point, so she was feeling good about her new living quarters.

I would meet Jennifer every few days for breakfast in the restaurant and bring her supplies like clothes and money. There was a shared kitchen, but Jen said she ate most of her meals out because people would steal the food.

After several weeks, she finally allowed me to go upstairs to her "space." I would like to say "room," but it was just a space separated from the next space by sheets hanging up. Each space contained a single bed, a dresser, and a night stand. My heart sank as I looked around. I couldn't imagine living in this type of place no matter how bad life was. It was one step up from a crack house. It was renting a "bed," but Jennifer assured me it was fine.

Jennifer wasn't working, and she felt that she couldn't keep having her parents support her with rent money. I didn't ask her to move back in with me because I knew I couldn't be home to monitor her so no good would come from that. She explained that she was about to be hired for a job, and then she would be able to get a better place. I exchanged money in her hand for her laundry which I did for her each week throughout most of those years! Having fresh laundry always made someone feel better, and I felt it was the least I could do.

It wasn't long until Jennifer relapsed again. And again. And again. And again. Each time was a repeat--detox, rehab, half-way house, programs and meetings--it seemed endless and totally draining. After one of Jennifer's relapses, I had her admitted for the second time in a lovely facility located in Valley Forge, Pennsylvania. It was a 28-day program that was away from the city. I felt so much better when she was away from the surroundings that seemed to lunge out to her with temptation via drug dealers on the corners. Valley Forge was a suburb of Philadelphia. The grounds were beautiful--they even had a peacock in the yard. Of course, it didn't stop her from returning to a life of drugs after she was released from there, but I still had a sense of optimism going there to visit her.

When Jennifer was released, I found a nice room for rent in my neighborhood that was bright and cheerful. I also was able to find a job for her not too far away so she would be able to pay her rent. Things seemed to be going well for a while. I would see Jennifer three or four times a week. After a few months, I noticed that she was losing weight. That was always a bad sign. Jennifer, like me, had a weight problem. She was always overweight which made me empathize with her struggle even more. I knew what it felt like to be fat. I had been fat my entire life except for two years when I had a terrible eating disorder.

Jennifer acted proud about her weight loss. She told me that she had decided to eat healthier because she was having trouble with her asthma carrying around so much weight. Of course, it seemed logical. She acted perfectly straight. That was one thing about Jennifer. She was a wonderful actress. I never could tell when she was high. I'm not sure if it was because she stayed away from me when she was really high or because she just knew how to control her appearance better. I think what fooled me also was living with my brother who was always looked stoned and drugged.

I was always looking to help (or others would call it "enable") Jennifer the best way that I could. Sometimes she would ask to borrow my car to get to work. In the hot weather, I would lend it to her because I could get to work with a friend. One day during this period, I received a call from her dad telling me that Jennifer had an accident. My heart went through my chest in panic, but he said she was okay--the car wasn't. Okay--you can always fix a car, but you can't always fix a life of someone in an accident. I was relieved--but angry. Why was Jennifer on a stretch of the highway when she was supposed to be at work?

Jennifer's dad picked her up and brought her to his house where I met them. He insisted that she be drug tested, and I agreed. Before I arrived at his home, I went to the drugstore and bought a drug testing kit that covered a wide range of drugs. While her dad was waiting for me to arrive with the kit, Jennifer went across the street to the convenience store to pick up some cigarettes because her nerves were bad.

When I got there, she took the bottle into the bathroom to urinate, and when she finished, she brought it to us so her father could test it with the testing strip. You can't imagine how relieved we both were when the testing strip came out "negative" for drugs. We hugged Jennifer while apologizing for accusing her of using drugs. I felt so guilty thinking that she finally was pulling it together for a few months and I was doubting her. Even though I had to buy another car, I knew it wasn't drugs that caused the accident. When Jennifer was going through her longest clean period a year later, she confessed to me that she had gone to the store not to buy cigarettes but rather apple juice. She diluted it with water in order to would take away the apple odor, and neither her father nor I thought to "smell" it. She told the story to me laughing because she knew she fooled us again.

It wasn't long after the accident that Jennifer lost her job. She claimed the job was much too disorganized...difficult...stressful...and not for her. She wasn't looking right to me, and I asked her what was causing that "drugged-out look" if it wasn't drugs. She explained that her doctor she was seeing for depression increased her meds and it was causing her to be drowsy and not focus. I wasn't happy, but now it made sense why she was unable to keep her job. I told her to call him and say the medication was too strong, but she replied that he explained that it takes a few weeks to level out. I agreed to cover her expenses for a few weeks until things got better.

Shortly after that conversation, things started going downhill again. I knew Jen was relapsing when her brother called me to tell me about a confrontation they had in the middle of a shopping area across from her rooming house. Jennifer was very close with her brother. Jason was born with a rare genetic disease that took his life at the age of 23. During his childhood, he had over 25 painful hospitalizations; after 18 he had five additional ones but eventually he lost his last battle.

He had always looked up to his sister as his hero, but over the time of her addiction, he distanced himself from her because it hurt him to see his sister this way. One day during that downhill slide, I asked him to visit Jennifer and gave him $20.00 to buy lunch for both of them because she said she was hungry. When Jason paid for their lunches, there was five dollars and some change left over. Jennifer demanded that he give her the change, but Jason refused. He said that his dad warned him not to give her any money because he believed she was using drugs again. Her dad feared what she would do with it. Right in the middle of the street outside the restaurant, Jennifer lunged at Jason screaming at him to give her the money, and when he wouldn't give it to her, she knocked him to the ground and took it. I then knew what was happening--drugs.

Once again, I called around looking for a place where Jennifer could get clean. She knew that it was time when I told her to go or we will all cut you off. I appealed to Valley Forge because she seemed to do so well there on her first visit. During her second visit, her counselor called me to suggest that Jennifer go to Florida because Philadelphia was tempting her too much to use drugs. He reinforced the theory of "people, places, and things," a common phrase used in recovery. They warn you to stay away from any past person, place, or thing that could trigger a relapse.

The counselor told me about a rehab called Awakenings in Boca Raton, Florida. He believed that if Jen were to go to a totally different environment away from the city to do her long-term rehabilitation, she had a better chance of recovering. I looked up the facility's website on the computer, and it looked beautiful. I knew that Boca Raton was one of the more elite areas of Florida where people did not hang out on street corners. The program was expensive, but I was reassured that after the first few weeks of intensive recovery support, Jennifer would be allowed to work and pay her own way for expenses. This was important because Awakenings was not a "funded" program by the government--this was a private program paid for by the family. The rent was $300.00 a week, and that did not include food. There were also additional expenses for laundry, transportation, and other personal items. I told Jennifer I cover the initial investment for a few weeks, but then she would need to find employment.

We went to visit the facility, and after talking to the director, I felt optimistic *once again* that this might be the solution to the problem. I was apprehensive about Jennifer being so far away from home, but I talked myself into believing it was like she was going away to college. I felt reassured when we arrived seeing that the streets were not lined with drug dealers standing there waiting to tempt vulnerable recovering addicts.

Boca was a beautiful place--very spread out and spacious. The rooms didn't quite look like the pictures on the website; however, they were far nicer than the cluttered half-way houses Jennifer had previously lived in. The facility was set up as apartments with two girls sharing a bedroom and two bedrooms in each apartment. Jen had to go to intensive outpatient therapy for the first three weeks before she would be allowed to go to work. I was told that the girls usually have a job within a few weeks so they could support themselves. In Jen's case, it took nearly two months before she found a job working for a credit card company.

As I've stated throughout this story, Jennifer was very smart. She was able to successfully "rob" the bank for over $5,000 and not get caught. Now as a sales person for a credit card company working on commission, she was able to get promoted to a supervisory position within the first two months. Her commission and salary was nearly $500.00 a week after taxes. Was she earning the money legitimately for this? Of course not. They had to call people to do a survey, and she was calling everyone she knew do the survey--including me. Since the company thought they were getting more surveys completed than ever, she was allowed to hire girls from Awakenings who also participated in her scam.

With so much money coming in, it was only a matter of time until Jennifer fell down again. And within two months of the new job, she did. The problem of not having drug dealers nearby on the streets was easily resolved. In Boca, the dealers were very accommodating and “delivered” to your location as if it were Pizza Hut To Go.

After two months of working at the job, Jennifer called me to say she was leaving the house to move in with some friends. She felt Awakenings was so expensive, and she could spend 1/3 the amount by moving with friends to their own house so she could have her own room. She called asking me to borrow some money while convincing me that these were “recovery” friends. She was in between pay-checks (so she claimed) and needed the money to put down on the house they would be sharing. She had just paid her rent for the month at Awakenings, and she said she would lose it if she left--but she would take the loss.

The number she gave me to contact her was a hotel, but she claimed they were staying there for a week until the house was ready for them to move in. It didn’t sound quite right--but I not only *wanted* to believe--I *needed* to believe she was telling me the truth. I wasn’t mentally up to another fall, and so I sent her a few hundred dollars that she promised to “repay” the following week.

By the following week, Jennifer was calling to tell me that the people robbed her of all of her money and belongings. If we (her dad or I) didn't send her money, she would be forced to stay on the beach under the boardwalk to sleep. She told me she had already been picked up and arrested for prostitution two days earlier and released until her hearing.

I will never forget because this was the week of Thanksgiving. My son, ex-husband, and I went out to Thanksgiving dinner together due to the stress we were all feeling. None of us were up to making a nice Thanksgiving dinner or being with other extended family members. My mother had died eight months earlier, and with the turmoil going on with Jennifer, I wasn't in the mood to socialize.

While we were on the way to the restaurant, Jennifer called us every five to six minutes threatening us to send money or she would harm herself...prostitute herself...jump into the water and drown herself...steal money and hurt someone...the threats were endless. I was so distraught that we were once again back to where we started from one more time.

Jennifer's father said the only thing he would do was send a bus ticket for her to return if she agreed to go to rehab. I guess in her desperation, she agreed. Two days later, Jennifer was home and on her way back to rehab again. This would be her third visit to Livengrin, a lovely rehab located in the outskirts of the city. I was hoping they would take her one more time because she seemed to achieve some limited success while she was there before.

It seemed that once again, Jennifer turned a corner--and I was so thrilled. I visited her weekly after attending the mandatory meeting for families in order to visit. She seemed calmer, more at peace, and more in touch with herself. She really thought that she would be ready to take the steps to finally recover.

I met with her counselors several times while she spent the month at the facility. They, too, felt Jennifer was really doing well. When it was almost time to leave, Jennifer told me about a private "clean house" run by a woman in Kensington. She said I could go with her to visit, and the woman was receptive to her living there. Jen would be eligible to receive a welfare check for nine months--the limit for people in recovery--and that money would go for her rent. By the time her welfare benefits ran out, she would be strong enough in her recovery to get a job and support herself. In these homes and programs, the food stamps were pooled for the group to do bulk buying. She would just need help with toiletries, clothes, and a carton of cigarettes each week.

We went to visit the house, and the nine or ten women rooming there were nice. The owner, who did not live on the premises but stayed during the day regularly, said she was very strict. The women had to go to daily Narcotic Anonymous (NA) meetings, and they were drug tested randomly on a regular basis. If there was one bad urine, they had to leave. Jennifer seemed to be in her best state of mind since her addiction started, so once again, I was feeling full of optimism and hope.

This house had an open policy for phone calls and visiting, so I was able to keep in touch with Jennifer daily and visit her regularly. I could take her out to shop or dinner as long as the manager was informed ahead of time. I was proud of Jen when she told me she was leading some of the NA meetings a few weeks later. I knew she had the traits of a born leader, and seeing her lead in a positive way added more hope to my jaded thinking.

Within three months, Jennifer called me sounding very excited. She was doing so well in her recovery that the owner of the house asked her to be the manager. The job had a lot of responsibility, but it also had a lot of perks. The responsibilities would include processing new women into the house, taking them to welfare to get situated for cash and food stamps, collecting rent, and making sure that anyone who was high or caught with a dirty urine was thrown out immediately. The perks seemed good. First, her rent would be paid. Next, she would have her own room. Best of all, she would be allowed to have an air conditioner which was great because she had bad asthma. This would allow her to breathe better when the sweltering heat would hit in July and August.

Jennifer seemed excited. We went out to dinner to celebrate and to buy the air conditioner for the bedroom which was located in the basement. It seemed as if things were finally going well. I was starting to relax and feeling like I could exhale. After a couple of months as manager, Jennifer told me that she met someone she cared about. The young lady, Raina, was a few years older than her. She told me they met at an NA meeting and had so much in common. Raina was also the manager of a recovery house, and she had a longer clean time than Jennifer.

I wasn't happy about Jennifer getting involved in a relationship when she had barely been clean for six months, and I reminded her how the recovery movement advises against relationships in the first year with others who are in recovery because when it comes to recovery, the formula is two positives can quickly become a negative. They are both vulnerable, and together they think they are superwomen who won't go back to how they were. It rarely works that way of course.

On August 23, 2001, Jennifer came to my job at lunchtime. I worked for a major social service organization in Philadelphia. I started working there when Jennifer was only five-years-old, so people watched her grow up. They also watched her destruction with drugs first hand through me because we were a family oriented organization where people really cared about each other. I remember that date because we were celebrating a co-workers birthday--the same day as my youngest sister's--by having a cook-out. While I was eating, Jennifer popped in and surprised me. I asked her why she was there in the middle of the day. I knew she couldn't just leave the rehab when she felt like it--she was the manager.

She went on to tell me that she and Raina had decided they were going to get a place together. She had gotten in trouble with the owner because she stayed out a couple of nights later than she had permission to do in order to be with Raina. Now the owner said she wanted Jennifer out because she had broken the rules. She also said the director suspected her of using drugs which was ridiculous. She had been clean for nearly seven months. I was so shaken. I told Jennifer I would call the owner to see what could be done.

The owner was nice, but firm about Jennifer leaving. She was upset about the house being left without supervision, but she was more upset because she believed that Jennifer had relapsed. She was willing to give her one more chance, but just as a resident--not as the manager. Jennifer said she wouldn't stay where she was being accused of using drugs when her only mistake was staying out an extra two hours with her new girlfriend. She said she was leaving and asked if she could stay at my house for a few days until she found a place to stay.

I was very apprehensive, but once again, I believed my daughter was doing so well. I wanted her to think I believed in her and supported her recovery efforts. I told her she could stay with me for a few days until she found an apartment. The search for a new place to live began immediately. I was too worried about leaving Jennifer alone in my house just in case I was wrong.

Within three days, Jennifer found an apartment in Kensington that she and Raina wanted to move into. She said the rent was $300.00 a month which they would split. Jennifer was just hired for a new job doing marketing in supermarkets where people would sign up for a free raffle for a prize in order for the company to get leads for a mobile phone company. I wasn't happy about the location of the apartment--back to Kensington--but Jennifer reassured me that all of her meetings and "clean friends" were there. I went to look at the apartment which was a third floor walk up. There was a shared bathroom in the hallway, but that didn't phases either of the girls because in "rehab living," this was typical. The room was furnished with a bed, dresser, table and chair. There were no cooking facilities, so I bought a Microwave and small refrigerator to get them started.

It was now early September of 2001. Jennifer was working and supposedly Raina was working as well. Several days a week when they were off from work, I let them both hang out at my house while I went to work so they could do their laundry. It was still hot outside, and in early September, I wanted Jennifer at least to be comfortable during the days when she was home from working with my air conditioning. I still gave her my car to go to work a few days a week because the job was at the other end of the city, and she was working in the evening. Coming home on public transportation late at night wasn't safe, and as long as I thought Jennifer was "clean," I didn't mind helping her.

On September 10, 2001, Jennifer told me she wasn't feeling well and came to my house. She was having trouble breathing following an attack of asthma. I called 911 because I was so worried about her not being able to breathe if I took her to a hospital. I felt they would have the equipment to quickly treat her sooner than I would be able to get her to the emergency room. Within a few minutes they arrived, treated her immediately, and took her to the hospital where they admitted her.

I vividly remember driving to visit her early the next morning and turning on my car radio as the announcer was shouting that the World Trade Center had been attacked by an airplane. I drove quickly to the hospital to watch the unfolding tragedy because my aunt, who was my mother's younger sister, was scheduled for open-heart surgery that morning less than a mile away from the bombing at New York University Hospital. At the same time, Jennifer's lung collapsed leaving her gasping for breath and in great pain. When it came to pain killers, I felt bad--but I told the hospital she was an addict. She could only have non-narcotic pain killers. I felt so bad because she was suffering, but I knew as soon as a narcotic went through her body, that would be it, and she would suffer even more as her body would crave the narcotic. After a week in the hospital, she was doing better and released. She stayed at my house for the day and then went home with Raina.

Sometime in mid-October, I started getting suspicious that something was going wrong. Jennifer started asking me for money again claiming that her pay checks were being held up. She said her rent was due, and neither she nor Raina had enough to pay it. They were both overspending on eating out without realizing they would be getting into this bind. I was a little apprehensive, but I gave her the money.

A few days later, her father told me that he was missing two rings that had been in his jewelry box. Of course, I was angry for his accusing her because she hadn't even been to visit him in a while. He was insistent that Jennifer had taken the rings in the upcoming days, but I couldn't understand how. He was usually home, and she didn't have a key.

Once the idea was in my head of her dad's missing jewelry, something made me think about looking at my jewelry collection that I kept in a wooden jewelry chest in my living room. Through the years, I had accumulated over $8,000 worth of gold jewelry and diamonds from my mother, grandmother, and a friend. I didn't wear jewelry as a rule, so I put it away in my jewelry chest. I always looked at it as my security blanket in case of a family emergency since my savings were now non-existent. I went running to the chest to look. Everything was gone. Everything--including a gold charm bracelet my mother had left me with charms for each one of her five children's births. I went crazy. I couldn't believe that Jennifer would rob me of everything I owned over those six weeks that I trusted her in my home.

In despair, I called her father, and we decided to confront her together. We went to her apartment and banged on the door. Both Jennifer and Raina were sleeping in bed and must have been startled. Jennifer got up and opened the door. Her father started opening her dresser drawers and sure enough--there were the needles and drugs. At that moment, I felt so defeated as if I was punched right in the stomach. I felt like vomiting and started shaking.

As her father kept going through everything in the apartment, he found a receipt from a pawn shop for the two rings that were stolen from his house. Jennifer admitted to pawning them as well as pawning my jewelry. She pawned her father's jewelry locally, so we went there with the ticket to get it back. I was not as lucky. My jewelry was sold in Atlantic City--where Jennifer drove my car to in order to sell it without telling me--and it was gone. She also stole my brother Lance's guitar from my house and pawned that, but her dad was able to retrieve it. That was my breaking point.

Throughout the years, many people talked to me about "tough love," but I never understood how they did it. I would think, "If my child is drowning, no matter what--I have to try to save her." And that's what I did. No matter how many disappointments and relapses Jennifer went through, I was there to pick up the pieces. She was my baby--the child I held in my arms and rocked to sleep. She was the girl who flung her arms around me saying, "I love you, Mom. You're the best mother in the world." Even though she was a woman, she was still my child.

Now I had to look with her with different eyes. Now I finally understood how those parents who talked to me about tough love felt when they had to cut the ties. I finally realized that all of my time, energy, and finances that went into Jennifer's "recovery" were still going up her arms. Standing in her apartment before leaving, I said, "This is it Jennifer. I can't do it anymore. If you want to be a drug addict, you will have to pay for it. I will not contribute to your addiction. Do not ask me for anything anymore. You can't come to my house, you can't use my car, and I will not help you until you are ready to go into a program." And I meant it. She said she loved me and she understood.

The next few months are a blur. Practicing the tough love was tough--especially on me--but it was reinforced when my Blockbuster movie account was charged with nearly $200.00 in fees within one week. I found out when I tried to rent a movie but was told my account was frozen due to non-payment. I couldn't believe that Jennifer would still steal from me after I cut her off, so I went to the store to talk to the manager. He said he had tapes of every transaction and looked up the dates and times to show me. Sure enough, there was Jennifer taking out the games and movies. No doubt she could sell them for a few dollars. I was so angry.

I would like to say that tough love seemed to be tougher on me than on Jennifer. I really admire people who can do it long term. I'm not sure if I could have. I went through so many emotional highs and lows. I remember hearing how I should have practiced tough love with my brother instead of enabling him. I had to live with that guilt for so many years wondering if I could have saved him by booting him into the street to fare for himself. But that was my brother. A guy could survive better on the street. Jennifer was my daughter. How could I walk away from her?

On the other hand, I finally understood that I couldn't save her at least on an intellectual level. She had to save herself. It wasn't a matter of my pulling her up--it was a matter of both of us drowning or me saving myself. At the time I said I would no longer help her, I finally felt as if I had to save myself because I was sinking.

"Saving myself" was very exhausting physically and emotionally. I became fanatical about waking up at 5:00 a.m. each day to listen to the news. I would turn on the news station as soon as the broadcast started and listen to hear if any young women had been found beaten or dead. I would hold my breath hoping not to hear any reports, and then go back to bed for an hour or two feeling relieved. If I didn't hear from Jennifer for four or five days, I would drive around her neighborhood trying to find her. She said she had moved, and I didn't know where she moved to. It could have been a crack house for all I knew. I was trying to keep my distance the best I could, but each day was a new day of torture of not knowing where she was or what was happening to her.

Two weeks before her 22nd birthday in February, Jason called me at work to tell me that Jennifer had called their father's house saying she had tried to commit suicide by cutting her wrist. Her father picked her up and brought her to his house where I met him. It had been nearly four months since I had last seen her. Looking at her, I felt disgusted for the first time. She had lost 30 pounds. Her arms were covered with needle marks, some which were infected. It appeared as if Jennifer had made a "weak" suicide attempt due to Raina leaving her after a very volatile fight. She said with Raina gone, she didn't want to live.

Raina called me the next day to tell me that she left because Jennifer's habit was out of control. It was up to $120.00 a day. Jen was acting very horribly to her expecting her to do more (stealing and prostitution) to bring more drugs to Jen. Raina told me that on one of her "excursions" on the avenue, she had been picked up by a thug and taken to another state where she was beaten and left on the road. She said she had to leave because Jennifer was worse than ever, and she couldn't deal with her fits of rage and physical bullying anymore.

One thing about Raina--she truly loved Jennifer. I'm not sure if she was gay or bisexual. I understand she went with men before she met Jennifer. She was four years older and had some more life experience. I heard a year after Jen's death that Raina was involved with a man, so I don't know. But when she was with Jennifer, she loved her as much as anyone could. She was willing to sell herself to get Jennifer a fix. That's love.

While Raina was selling herself to help Jennifer, Jennifer's best friend, Trisha, was trying everything she could to help her. With her own money, she took Jennifer to a doctor who was supposed to have a series of shots to stop the need for drugs. Trisha was a true friend to Jennifer since high school where they bonded as bullies! Trisha would never let anyone push her around, so Jennifer respected her for that. Trisha was always trying to save Jennifer from her addiction, but Jennifer couldn't save herself.

Taking the suicide threat seriously, I took Jennifer to Friend's Hospital which was the psychiatric facility in our area. There she would be evaluated and sent out to detox and rehab again. It was the week of her birthday, and yet I could find no joy in it knowing how and where she would be spending it. She was transferred to a detox/rehab called Kirkbride in the West Philadelphia section of the city. It wasn't my choice, but it was the only place willing to take a suicidal drug addict who needed to detox.

I called Jennifer daily. On her birthday two days later, I asked a friend to deliver her clean laundry to the rehab with a birthday card, a carton of cigarettes, and $25.00. Jennifer was going to be there for five or six days, and then she had to transfer to a rehab program or leave. I told her that I knew of two long-term programs that would be happy to take her. They were programs I worked with through my job, and they were always willing to open their doors for her. She agreed that she would go, and once again, I felt a sense of relief.

The program was going to send their van for her the next day. I told her I would call her first thing in the morning to make sure she had everything ready to go and also to say goodbye. Once she would enter the program, she would be on blackout again for a couple of weeks. On the following morning, my first call to her was at 7:30 a.m. There was no answer. I called again at 8:00, 8:30, and 9:00 thinking maybe Jennifer was having breakfast or taking a shower. When she didn't answer by 9:30 a.m., I called her social worker.

I explained that I was trying to locate Jennifer because the van from the program was due to pick her up at 10 a.m. Then the social worker gave me the news that I refused to believe--Jennifer wasn't there. At first I thought the van came for her early, but she assured me it wasn't the van. Jennifer requested to leave on her own. The social worker had to give her a bus token to leave as part of their policy.

I was freaking out. I asked how she could let her leave in as much as she was suicidal. She replied the psychiatrist had determined she was not suicidal. I asked how she could just walk out on her own. She reminded me at 22, she was an adult and could make her own decisions. I hung up the phone with my heart palpitating and threw up.

I don't know why it hit me so hard, but it did. Maybe it was because now I knew there would be no hope. I cried uncontrollably for several hours and called out from work that day. I felt as if my grieving period had officially started.

Jennifer left me a message on the telephone the next day. She said, "Hi Mom. I'm really sorry that I had to go, but I just couldn't do the program. Raina and I are back together, and we are doing fine. I'll call you soon, but I don't want you to worry about me. I am sorry I disappointed you, but I just couldn't do it. I love you."

Five weeks went by before I heard from Jennifer again. Jennifer would call me every week or so, usually around 2:00 a.m. Drug addicts have no sense of time when they are getting high. I learned that over the years between my brother and my daughter. One time she called crying because she was scared when a man held a gun to her head and robbed her money. I knew she was cruising on Frankford Avenue prostituting herself for a hit. Each time she called, I would ask her if she was ready to get clean and tell her I'd pick her up. She was never ready although she always promised to phone me the next day after she would think about it. Those calls never came.

In between her phone calls, I drove through the streets of Kensington every few days, visited places where she used to hang out, called phone numbers of people who knew her just to check if anyone had seen her--and found out practically nothing. I was feeling so hopeless, but then she would leave me a message that she was doing fine.

She made sure to call when I was at work to leave a message so she wouldn't need to have that "talk" with me about being ready to recover.

The following week, at 2:00 a.m. the phone rang. I jolted up to get it thinking, "Finally." It wasn't "finally," but rather "final." It was the hospital calling to tell me Jennifer was there in critical condition. They refused to talk to me any further until I got there even though I was screaming at them, "Is my daughter alive? Is she alive?" I called her father and within 10 minutes we were on our way for that torturous twenty minutes ride. So many things were running through my mind.

When we went into the hospital, the staff called us into the private room and told us Jennifer had died. They said she was dead when she arrived at the hospital, and they had done their best to revive her with no luck. It was a combination of an asthma attack combined with the heroin. Raina was at the hospital hysterical. She called 9-1-1 as soon as she saw Jennifer couldn't catch her breath.

The nightmare was over. Over for Jennifer. Over for the rest of us. It was a double edged sword. On one hand, my daughter was dead. There was no longer any false hope. On the other hand, there was just no hope. She was *not* going to be that "one in a hundred to recover" as I believed on that first night of her revelation. At least she wasn't killed in violence. No one knifed her to death or beat her to death which was always my greatest fear.

Nearly 30 people from the Kensington recovery community attended Jennifer's funeral. It was amazing to listen to the stories they shared with me about how Jennifer saved their lives. They truly loved her and grieved for her. That was the side of Jennifer I loved--my little girl who would help people when they were hurting and always with a hug or encouraging words.

Raina also grieved for Jennifer deeply. She did her best to take care of Jennifer even under the most hideous of conditions. I don't know what happened to her in future years, but I hope her life turned around.

One thing I learned through this experience is that recovery is a life-time battle. Very few people really achieve it. I heard stories of people who were clean for years who relapsed and died. It's a dark world with only fleeting light for most people who are addicts.

Once their spark flickers out, those who loved them must find the peace that couldn't be found during their loved one's addiction. They are out of their pain, and now it's time for us to heal from ours.

The grieving process is exactly that--a process that takes time. You'll know that you've reached the end of the cycle when you get to the point of acceptance. That means you can stop questioning and blaming yourself and your child--just accept it as one of life's greatest tragedies.

Rest in peace Jennifer. Rest in peace to all of the beautiful children that parents have lost to a world that was inconceivable to us.

Jennifer Needle in Her Arm

CHAPTER FOUR

LYNNE ABRAHAM'S LETTERS

When Jennifer's addiction became a reality to me, I didn't understand how a teenager had such easy access to drugs. I really believed that if the "authorities" knew about this, they would stop it. Several weeks after Jennifer entered Fresh Start, in my desperation, I wrote a letter to a woman named Lynne Abraham who was then the District Attorney of Philadelphia. I was feeling very desperate at this point, so I tried to reach out to anyone I thought could help me. This is a copy of the letter:

March 19, 1999
Dear Ms. Abraham,

I know that you are one of the busiest people in this city, but I hope you will indulge me for just a couple of minutes in a matter that I think is life and death.

My name is Bonnie Kaye, and I live in Northeast Philadelphia. Last year, my daughter Jennifer was a senior at Northeast High School. Her first assignment for her senior English class was to write an essay on the person she admired the most. You were her hero. It was a beautiful essay about how she admired your work as a district attorney, and how she now wanted to become an attorney for her career. It was an "A" paper that the teacher kept, or I would have sent it to you.

I was so proud of Jennifer because she had a troubled life as a teenager. She was involved in a gang here in the Northeast during her tenth and eleventh grade years. She pulled herself out of the gang before eleventh grade ended. I really thought she was on the right track, and the essay she wrote about you was so inspirational that I thought all the hard years of parenting that I and her father had put in had finally paid off.

Jennifer won a scholarship to Community College of Philadelphia (CCP), and we were thrilled when this was announced at her graduation in June. Throughout the summer she vacillated about starting school and finally decided that she wanted to wait, get a job, and get her own apartment. I accepted her decision because I was a late bloomer myself--a high school dropout that did not return to school until my 30's. I am also a GED instructor at CCP (part-time) and I know that not everyone is ready for college at a young age. And so Jennifer found a job and moved into a nearby apartment.

During the summer, she started to go to a club called Space in Center City. This is a "rave" club for teenagers and young adults targeted for 17 – 24 year olds. She started showing erratic behavior patterns and became a regular at the club. There is no drinking allowed there, but I later found out that there is a lot of drugging there. Unfortunately, I found out too late. Eight weeks ago, several days before Jennifer turned 19, she revealed that she was using heroin.

For the last eight weeks, our lives have been in total turmoil trying to undo this horrible nightmare.

Jennifer is currently in a halfway house after detoxing twice including one overdose three weeks ago. She had developed a $50.00 a day habit over the seven months that she was using this deadly drug. I am trying to be optimistic, but I am also realistic. I don't know if my daughter will make it. Addiction is a lifelong battle. I know. My brother died from a drug habit after a 20-year addiction.

I am not soliciting your sympathy as the district attorney. I am sure your office is filled with cases involving drugs and addicts. What does concern me is that there is a club that solicits teens where drugs run rampant. I have questioned other people about this club, Space, and have been told that the owners are not only aware of what is going on, but also partake in these activities.

Ms. Abraham, please understand that I am not saying that anyone forced my daughter to start using drugs. She decided to take that step. In fact, her crowd of friends all started to do heavy drugs once they started going to that club. Drugs are sold in the club because teenagers are easy targets to prey on.

Is there anything you can do to stop this club in its tracks? If one teenager can be saved by your effort, it will be worth the world to some unsuspecting parents who may have a chance of keeping their child alive.

I appreciate your reading this letter, and please let me know if you can help.

With sincere admiration for your courage,
Bonnie Kaye

Two days later, Ms. Abraham called me at my home to express her concern for Jennifer. I was so amazed that this busy woman would take the time to call me, a total stranger, who was reaching out to find some hope.

A little over a year later, I sent her this letter:

June 11, 2000
Dear Ms. Abraham,

Last March, I wrote to you about my daughter, Jennifer, who was a heroin addict. In that letter, I expressed my anger about the teen club, Space. You were so kind and gracious in calling me and offering me words of support. You also assigned your assistant to see how he could help.

Now, fifteen months later, I would like to give you a brief update. Since last March, Jennifer has relapsed five times. I have been through the maze of detox units, mental health facilities, rehabs, and halfway houses. She has overdosed three times but miraculously been brought back to life. I recently sent her to a program in Florida as her very last chance before I wash my hands of the situation. I have spent over $13,000.00 this year trying to get her well. Money is never the issue when it comes to my children, but throwing money away is because I have landed at the same point where I started. I am sure you can imagine the heartbreak of a mother who sees her daughter continually falling into a dark hole. My daughter's heroin habit by the time she turns herself in each time is in excess of $100.00 a day. Can you imagine raising, nurturing, and loving a child since birth only to learn that she is prostituting herself on

Frankford Avenue to raise money for her habit? Ms. Abraham, I am a broken woman from this.

Anyway, enough of my tales of woe. I did not write to you looking for sympathy even though you were very generous in giving it to me when we spoke. I guess this is where I get pissed off. When I spoke to your assistant last year, he was kind, but insistent that unless my daughter gave him the information about the club, he couldn't do anything. Although I did ask my daughter on several of her more remorseful and sober occasions if she would provide this information, she refused fearing her life would be in danger. I gave him as much information as I was able to obtain from Jennifer and her friends, but he said that without their direct testimony, nothing much could be done. I find it somewhat sad that the whole police department can't send in undercover people to find the same drugs as my daughter and her friends find, but he claimed that wouldn't work. I gave up trying to close down the club after that.

So, here is my next question, Ms. Abraham. Can you explain to me how my underage daughter is able to find heroin on the streets so easily but the police are not able to stop this? My daughter developed a whole network of junkie friends in Philadelphia who all seem to be able to buy heroin on a daily basis to feed their habit. Is the issue that heroin is just not that big of a priority, or am I missing something?

Ironically, part of my job is to work with ex-offenders and recovering addicts to provide them with training and employment in an attempt to start their lives over. It seems that they were all able to access drugs with relative ease. What part of the big picture am I missing here? We both know that drugs are responsible for so many of the social problems that face our city, including violence, family dysfunction, and physical/mental health problems. These problems end up costing the taxpayers millions and millions of dollars each year. I would think putting an end to this nightmare would be high up on the agenda of priorities. And yet, from where I am sitting, this situation is allowed to prosper and flourish.

I am not so presumptuous to ask you why. I am sure you have some excellent responses that are certainly true. I am just tired, Ms. Abraham. This past year has been so mentally exhausting to me. I lost my devoted mother to lung cancer last month, I have a chronically ill son who has a rare immune deficiency disease that could kill him at any time, and I work normally 12 hours each day just to try to provide for my children as a single parent. Life under the best of circumstances is difficult. This extra-added wrench thrown in just pushes me closer to the edge of falling over.

Well, thanks at least for listening. You seem like a lovely, responsive woman. Perhaps someday I will have the chance to meet you in person. If not, I'll write to you again giving you an update.

Best regards,
Bonnie Kaye, M.Ed.

Again, I had a call back within a day or two. Ms. Abraham explained how they keep arresting drug dealers, but as soon as they take them off the corner, new ones appear within hours. They would keep trying.

My next letter was written two weeks before Jennifer's death. You can tell my desperation here during the period where Jennifer had disappeared.

March 30, 2002
Dear Ms. Abraham,

I have written to you several times since 1999 about my daughter Jennifer, now age 22, who is a heroin addict. You were very kind, compassionate, and responsive to my letters. Considering I am a complete stranger, I can't tell you how much that meant to me.

Now, three and a half years later since my initial shock, I am writing to you once more. I know you must be one of the busiest people in this city, but I feel as if you are my last hope. I'm not even sure why I feel compelled to write to you. Maybe it's because when Jennifer was a senior at Northeast High School in 1998, she wrote about you in her "A" paper of why you were the person she most admired. Maybe I am hanging on to that obscure connection and your proven compassion to write this letter of desperation.

My daughter is lost, Ms. Abraham. Since learning of her heroin addiction and originally writing to you about the drugs being sold to her at Space, I have now spent over $30,000 trying to rehabilitate my daughter. The money is not the issue because I'd give up everything I have if my daughter could recover. But the money, which depleted everything I owned, was thrown down the drain. I have sent Jennifer through numerous detoxes, rehabs, halfway houses, clean and sober programs, doctors, and therapists all for nothing. I even sent her to a program in Florida in hopes that being away from the city would be a help. That's when I still had an illusion that my daughter had returned to me from the depths of hell.

My daughter started going downhill this past August after her seven-month clean period. I was once again too stupid to see it, or maybe it's just because her lying is so perfected. Between September and November, she made the ultimate mistake and robbed me of all of my valuable possessions that had been left to me through the years by family members. This happened over a two-month period when I trusted her in my home alone because I thought she was doing so well. The monetary value was approximately $8,000.00, but the emotional value was much greater. This included a charm bracelet that my mother left me when she died two years ago with all of the charms of my siblings that she cherished. Jennifer also robbed her father during this time. Although Jennifer kept denying her involvement and swore she wasn't using drugs, I had to face the truth.

Her father and I went to her rented room in Kensington where she lived with her girlfriend and somehow got in and confronted her. There we found needles and reality struck--she was using heroin again. She finally admitted the story including robbing our possessions claiming that it wasn't her, it was the heroin. At that point I told her that she and the heroin were the same to me. I felt so betrayed and violated. Her father and I decided to practice tough love at that point for the first time. I couldn't keep doing this. It seemed like the more I gave Jennifer, the worse she got. So I broke the strings.

Since then, Jennifer kept in touch with me once a week or so. She went to detox a few more times, but then back to the streets. She started prostituting for her habit which grew to over $150 a day. One night in late January she called me at 2 a.m. crying because a man who she sold her body to held a gun to her head a robbed her of $80.00. She was so scared and frightened. I offered her the chance to go into a program, but she wasn't ready.

A night before her 22nd birthday on February 6, she slit her wrist. Her brother picked her up, and I arranged for him to take Jennifer to her father to take her into Friends Hospital. From November when I last saw her to February, she had lost about 30 pounds and had tracks up and down her arms. She also had abscesses on her body from the heroin needles. I was hoping this was a true call for help, but it wasn't. She detoxed again at Kirkbride and then disappeared after ten days. She left me a message a week later saying she was going to make it on her own and she loved me. She said she'd see me soon. That was the last I heard for five weeks. She finally called me again last week, telling me she's trying to beat her habit again and she'll see me soon.

In 1998, when my daughter graduated Northeast High School, she won a scholarship to college. If she had taken that route, she'd be graduating college this spring like her Northeast classmates. Maybe she'd be applying to law school as she had planned. Who knows, maybe she would have even someday worked for you, the person she admired the most. Ms. Abraham, Jennifer was so smart. She could have been an excellent attorney. Now she needs an attorney. Now she has a criminal record. She was arrested for prostitution in January and never showed up for her hearing. She is now a wanted criminal.

I am trying to cope with life although I constantly feel as if I am in a state of mourning. I am an administrator at a non-profit agency where I pride myself in helping people change their lives every day. Through the years, I have worked with hundreds of recovering addicts in their efforts to be free of addiction. I never did it with the thought that I'd be fighting my own personal battle with my daughter. Although I am a counselor by profession, I felt incapable of working through this alone and sought the expertise of many in this field. I have yet to find an answer to my daughter's problem.

Ms. Abraham, I don't know if you can understand this, but I hope you can. You help so many people each year and I know you have to feel good about that, much like the work I do that makes me feel good. But I feel that all of the good work I've done over the years in helping literally thousands of people put their lives on track is negated by the fact that I can't help my own daughter. It's a feeling of helplessness and powerlessness. It's a feeling of personal failure. All of the counseling and comfort that my colleagues have given me doesn't change that fact. I know it's not rational to feel this way, but when it's the child that you've loved, cherished, nurtured, and tried to guide through the years, rationality goes down the drain and emotion rules. I used to feel vulnerable because I couldn't protect my little girl from her bad dreams when she was sleeping in her crib. How do you think I feel now that she is living this nightmare?

I used to fear that my daughter would overdose. I used to fear that she would get AIDS or hepatitis. I don't even care about that anymore. Now my greatest fear is that she will meet a violent death from one of these men who she prostitutes with on a daily basis. And how many unsavory men do you think she has to do this with each day to support her habit? A part of me has already died just knowing this Ms. Abraham. I try to go through the days functioning. I work harder than ever trying not to think too much because if I did, I'd probably lose my sanity.

And so I am asking you once again if you can help me. I want my daughter back,

Ms. Abraham. I want to hold her again and kiss her and see if I can make it better one more time. I don't know where to turn or where to look. I don't know what to do. As each day goes by without hearing from her, I feel more desperate. Each time the phone rings, I jolt up thinking that it's bad news. Each time the phone doesn't ring, I keep wondering if Jennifer is being beaten or raped. I hate living this way. Please let me know if you have any ideas that might help me through this. Maybe if you could talk to her in person, it would make a difference. I'm the person she loved the most and it didn't help. But maybe since you're the person she admired the most, maybe it would make a difference.

Thank you again for taking the time to listen to the desperation of a frightened mother.

Sincerely,
Bonnie Kaye, M.Ed.

Two weeks later, Jennifer died. Ms. Abraham called me the day after her death to express how sad she was. She didn't have a chance to call me back after my last letter, but she said it was on her list--and I believe her.

A year later, a day before Jennifer's death day, the telephone rang and it was Lynne Abraham on the telephone. She called to tell me that she knew the following day would be the one-year anniversary of Jennifer's death. She was thinking of me and wanted to let me know. Can you imagine the District Attorney of a city the size of Philadelphia marking this on her calendar a year in advance? I was floored by her compassion and kindness, and I have never forgotten what it meant to me at that moment.

Several weeks later, I sent her this final letter.

May 3, 2003
Dear Ms. Abraham,

Please forgive this delayed letter. I started writing it to you several weeks ago, three days before Jennifer's unveiling and your phone call. I wanted to make sure to say things correctly, so I took the time I needed to finish it.

First, allow me to thank you for being so responsive to this desperate mother over the years. When I first wrote to you in the spring of 1999, I was very naïve about drugs. I was looking to place a blame for my daughter's addiction on someone or something other than her. Or, shall I say, in the upcoming years when I wrote to you, I was looking for someone or somewhere to put the blame on for my daughter's continual relapses. Your department sounded like a good place to start. It's also a good place to end this yearlong journey of mourning.

In this year, I have found myself going through the lowest of low moments blaming myself for Jennifer's death. I kept telling myself that after I started to practice tough love last November when she robbed me, her demise went steadily downhill. The truth, in retrospect, was that nothing I would have done within my power could have saved her. She was doomed. The addiction was too powerful for her to overcome.

I kept blaming the police for not arresting the drug dealers. And then I blamed your department for not prosecuting these dealers to the fullest, allowing them back on the streets again. The truth, in retrospect, is that no matter how many drug dealers you would have removed from the streets, it wouldn't stop drugs from returning to them quickly. Drugs are just too big of a business. It's beyond you and the police. I know you are trying as hard as anyone can. But in a world that is foreign to you and me, it's almost impossible to make a difference. Drug dealers are like those standing, vinyl blow-up punching bags with clown faces we used to play with when we were children. You knock them down, and they bounce back no matter how hard you punch or how many times.

Ms. Abraham, quite honestly, I have a sense of relief that Jennifer is now at peace. Her life was a tortured hell while she was using drugs. The hepatitis was killing her a little more each day. The danger of the streets was hovering over her head with violence surrounding her. I couldn't save her. This is the most difficult thing for a mother to accept. I tried so hard to protect my daughter over the years, even when she was wrong. Maybe that's what I did wrong. Maybe I should have let her fall sooner and understand the consequences of doing wrong things. But I didn't. I protected her because I always felt sorry for her and loved her. Even though Jennifer had a negative side, she also had a good side that was just as strong. That good side was truly caring and compassionate; she often helped those who were in need of help. She would have been an excellent counselor or human service worker if she had not been an addict. Throughout her addiction, during her clean times, she helped other addicts who were in worse shape than she was. She was well loved by many who mourned her death last year at her funeral, telling me how they wouldn't be there on that day without Jennifer's help.

Ms. Abraham, I wrote to you on three occasions during Jennifer's addiction. I was a total stranger to you, reaching out for help. Each time, you took the time to respond to me by phone calls or letters or both. You don't know how much that meant to me. While I was going through a parent's greatest nightmare, you reached out with kind words and good intentions. You did it quickly and with great concern and compassion. When I tell my family and friends how you called me the night before the unveiling, they were stunned that a stranger would take the time to do something so loving and thoughtful. This is who you are. It takes a lot to impress me because I work with so many outstanding people daily who are committed to changing the quality of life for others on a daily basis. But you, Ms. Abraham, stand right on the very top of this list.

If you know of anyone who is in need of support while he/she is going through this horrible situation, please feel free to refer them my way. I am strong enough at this point of time to give that support. I wasn't before.

With extreme gratitude,
Bonnie Kaye

Amazingly, two years after the death of Jennifer, I received this letter from Lynne Abraham:

May 6, 2004
Dear Bonnie:

I constantly think of you and Jennifer in the season of renewal. After all, we have come out of the season of chilly winds and bleak days into the glorious sun and fresh breeze of spring. With spring comes the release and lightening of the burdens we have suffered in the past.

Jennifer's life and death may, I hope, service in an odd kind of way as a test for you in the crucible. Only through adversity are we shaped and reshaped, strengthened and tempered, ready for whatever life may bring to us. I know this is you--resilient, ready, full of resolve.

Keep me in mind for any service I can offer to you. I am just a phone cord away from you.

Lynne

What a humanitarian! Two years later, she thought of me! To date, I still haven't had the opportunity to meet this wonderful woman. It seemed that our paths crossed a number of times moments before and after each other at events I attended to remember the children of drug addiction at rallies and vigils.

Before adding this material, I tracked down Mrs. Abraham at her private law practice to ask her permission to reprint my letters to her. I told her that I plan to give her a copy in person so we can finally meet. I am so looking forward to that day.

CHAPTER FIVE

OTHER WRITINGS

Several years after Jennifer's death, I was watching the soap opera "All My Children." I was an avid fan since their opening year when I was 19 years old. The soaps always brought me comfort because their problems were bigger than mine, and they managed to survive which inspired me.

There was a story line when the character Erica Kane, played by Susan Lucci, was going through her addiction to painkillers. I watched with pain as I hoped her outcome would be better than Jennifer's. The story was done with sensitivity and understanding to those who were going through addiction as well as their family members.

Another storyline came up when a new woman in town, Chrystal, questioned whether her 19-year-old daughter was using drugs. She wasn't--she was tricked into it--but her mom still wondered. The main male character of the show, Tad Martin, played by Michael Knight, made a comment that felt like a knife when through me when the same "stereotypical" remarks were made that I was used to hearing. I wrote this piece to address the writers and raise their consciousness as you'll see in my letter to them.

Even if you're not interested in soap operas, I know as a grieving parent you'll appreciate the sentiments here. I never did receive a response.

AN OPEN LETTER TO TAD MARTIN IN PINE VALLEY

I have watched the soap opera "All My Children" since 1971. I am a loyal fan and friend. I feel like the characters in Pine Valley really are my family because I am with them five times a week--more than any of my real family members. After 30 years, you get to know these characters and parallel your own life's trials and tribulations with theirs. I have had equal amounts if not more of heartache, heartbreak, and trauma as Erica Kane, the star of the show. I don't have her star quality beauty or number of ex-husbands, but I could give her a run for her money in all other areas of drama and trauma.

One of the reasons why I am attached to soap operas is because they reflect certain aspects of life as I see it and live it. This gives me a comfort zone in a world filled with my own harsh realities. Soaps energize me and inspire me by showing that even when you are really down, it doesn't mean that you are really out. Someday you will rise again and good times will overtake the bad memories.

Soap operas raise real life issues and awareness to the general public. A number of years ago, Erica Kane found herself addicted to prescription drugs after a back injury. It was a slow progression, but in time, the character resorted to disguising herself and hanging in back alleys looking to buy pills to support her out-of-control habit. There were lots of wake up calls and interventions by loving family members, and eventually, Erica went away into rehab and recovered. She learned from that experience that she could no longer even have one drink because of her addiction. Bravo, Erica. Bravo, All My Children. Erica did really well for years, often tempted during her most difficult moments to pick up a drink--but she never did--until this spring. After being rejected from her favorite daughter's life, Erica raised the glass, and as all people of addiction know, one drink is always too much, and no amount is enough or something along those lines. Erica went into an alcoholic stupor for weeks, and only family confrontation was able to make her face it and go back into treatment.

Now, just when I get finished praising All My Children for their sensitive way of bringing the plight of drug and alcohol addiction to the masses, they counteracted the good by making a VERY BIG BLUNDER. It really saddened me because here I thought we were so in synch with each other after 30 plus years. It was something that wouldn't have even caught my attention if I hadn't lived my own particular nightmare, so I'll assume the comments were made due to lack of education rather than lack of sensitivity.

My own personal tragedy occurred in April of 2002, when I lost my 22-year-old daughter, Jennifer, to a three-and-a-half year addiction to heroin. It was definitely the worst heartbreak in my life. Not only did I lose my daughter, but I lost her over a slow progression of deterioration of her mind and body. The little angel that I held in my arms as a baby grew up and had her body taken over by a monster demon that now had her shooting needles in her arms. Her body became possessed by a force stronger than the mountain of miracle workers, social workers, and do-gooders who were only able to help her to take her life back for short periods of time.

Any parent who losses a child knows the true meaning of the word "tragedy." But parents who lose their children to drugs have been living a private hell of our own before the actual death because our children are on a constant spiral downward and *we don't know how to save them.* And what contributes to the pain is the fact that we are so isolated in finding others who can understand our grief. We feel as if this is our "dirty little secret" that we can't tell for fear of others judging our children--and our *parenting skills.*

You see, we have been judging ourselves throughout this experience wondering what we have done wrong and where we failed as parents. It takes a long time of going through that self-blame because we are good parents. Bad parents don't question what they've done wrong, but good parents do. Some of us spend years or even lifetimes blaming ourselves for something that we had absolutely no control over. But when you lose a child, this is human nature.

When you lose a child to drugs, it's not like losing a child to a car accident or drive-by shooting. The grief is the same, but the aftermath is different. People are not viewed by society as bad parents because their children were victims of crime or accidents. But parents of addicts are different. People do view them differently. People look at us and think--and sometimes even verbalize--, "Didn't you have any control over your child? What kind of parent were you?" And if you think I'm overreacting, well, I'm not. Do you know how I know that? I know because up until the time that my daughter became a drug addict, *I thought the same thing.* Ouch. It hurts to say the truth, but I'd rather say the words that others are fearful of thinking in order to give them the courage to face their terrible feelings of guilt. There is great comfort in that old cliché "the truth will set you free," because facing my own personal demons in life have set me free from irrational feelings of guilt that we all go through.

Sorry for sidestepping for the moment, so let's return to my point about All My Children. There's a character in the storyline who has been around since his childhood. His name is Tab Martin. Through the years Tad has gone through some personality revision. He used to be known as "Tad, the Cad" because he was a womanizer from his late teenage years into adulthood; however, he was usually a likeable cad who had many redeeming qualities. The kind, loving, respectable Martin family adopted him as a 10-year old child after he was abused and tossed out of a car by his raging, psychotic father. Now, all of these years later as a devoted father and stepfather to two young men, he has gained a lot of credibility in Pine Valley.

He also has a new love interest, Crystal who recently joined the cast with her sexy 19-year-old daughter, Babe. When Babe nearly dies from an illegal drug slipped into her drink, Tad is there to console his new love interest. Crystal asks Tad if he thinks that Babe was capable of taking drugs. Here's the response, and I quote, *"Would she mess with drugs when she has a baby to raise at home? No, I don't think so. <u>I know you didn't raise her to be foolish or irresponsible</u>."* Actually it's an exact quote because I taped that episode not to misquote.

Ouch. It hurts because that statement reflects the feelings of too many people who have no clue of how hard you try to be a good parent *yet* the public perceives these good parents as *foolish* or *irresponsible*. It perpetuates the stereotype of a drug parent as being a *failure* as a mother or a father. It implies that *I must have done something wrong* along the way of raising my daughter because she did "*mess with drugs*." It's almost like I should be wearing a scarlet "F" on my body for FAILURE--AS IF I DON'T FEEL ENOUGH LIKE A FAILURE WITHOUT THE

CLUSTERED SIDEBARS OF PEOPLE REMINDING ME.

It is not unusual for parents who lose children to drugs to beat themselves up for the loss of their children for a myriad of reasons. Our minds are whirling with questions such as, *"What did I do that hurt my child so badly that he/she had to turn to drugs?"* or *"How could I have been so stupid that I didn't know my child was doing drugs?"* We spend years dissecting every one of our memories, good ones, bad ones, important ones, unimportant ones, and even ones that were buried very deeply just to see if we can figure out what life catastrophe could possibly have driven our children into a dark world that was foreign to us. This world included stealing, dealing, violence, and prostitution just to get a hit of something that would zombie them out. As parents of addicts, we were stretched to the mental limit of survival while our children robbed from us, violated us, acted out on us, and manipulated us emotionally with every lie imaginable just so we would help support their habit just one more time.

Although each of us feels the sense of social isolation, there are thousands of us each year joining the ranks of this group. We come from all walks of life, from all religions, nationalities, cultures, financial backgrounds, and occupations. Parents of addicts run the gamut from blue-collar workers to workers in blue--namely policemen and policewomen. In fact, my daughter's roommate at one of her rehabs was the daughter of our city's former police commissioner. When I kept doubting myself through those years, I felt a sense of comfort because I wasn't doubting the police commissioner. There was no thought in my mind that he was bringing up his daughter to be "foolish or irresponsible." Not by a long shot.

Often, parents who lose children to drugs are silent mourners. They are afraid to say how or why their children died to family, friends, neighbors and coworkers, making up reasons such as "heart-attacks" or "seizures." How do I know that? I know it first hand from my own mother who covered up my brother's death with the "heart attack" excuse. In 1987 at the age of 33, my brother died from narcotics after 20 years of abuse. My brother was one of five children and the only drug abuser. He was not brought up any differently than me or my other siblings. At no point was he given a message by either of my parents that drugs were okay. On the contrary. As soon as my father realized what was going on, he tried everything from soft love to tough love. He had our family attending Synanon group meetings in California hoping to find the answers to problems that were first surfacing in America in the mid 1960's. Drugs were new to our society--an unknown force of evil that took over the culture like, excuse the cliché, a "Bat out of Hell." All those catchy expressions like "turn on and tune out" became realities for thousands of people who found that tuning out often meant going out--for good.

In the 1960's and 70's, our rock heroes were lighting their fires and then having them snuffed out via overdosing. Drugs were glamorized because they allowed people to reach new levels of "mystic crystal revelations." Everyone was doing them. Well, everyone hip was doing them. The Beatles were doing them. The Rolling Stones were doing them. Others were doing them and dying from them. Janis Joplin died from them. Jimmy Hendrix died from them. Jim Morrison died from them. And even though the loss of our musical idols hit hard, it wasn't hard enough for people to say STOP. People just kept doing them.

Not everyone who did drugs became addicts. In fact, most people *never* became addicts. They were "recreational" drug users--party people. But they functioned in a world of reality in between the high times. They had jobs they attended daily; families that they were responsible to; bills that were paid on time or nearly on time. They faced life on life's terms. But there were those that never got past the state of being high. They lived for it, and all of their daily maneuvers were focused around getting the next high--no matter what the cost.

We never understood my brother's addiction. None of us viewed it as a disease. All of us were annoyed by it. My brother was a charming, personable, handsome man, short of statue with a happy-go-lucky nature and great sense of humor. He was born with an innate sense of intelligence that as a youth, allowed him to never pick up a book to study but to always to achieve high scholastic grades. Unfortunately, he not only never reached *his* potential, but actually reached *no* potential because he was drug-driven from the age of 13. He loved being high. He never tried to mask it, hide it, or excuse it. He was an honest addict. He had no intention of recovering because he never considered his addiction to be a problem--at least not to him. He regarded it as "our" problem because he was happy living high.

Back in the days of my brother's addictions, we were clueless. All roads to help led to nowhere. We just kept getting angry and yelling a lot. My brother spent 17 years of his drug life in California where my father resettled after my parents divorced, and when he burned every last bridge there, he came back here to Philadelphia where he spent the remaining three years of his life living with me. Actually, let me rephrase that. He spent the last three years of his life staying with me and being high.

I didn't understand why my brother had this need to be stoned day in and day out, but I accepted it. There didn't seem like much of anything I could do would change it. He worked, supporting his habit for the most part, and in spite of his addiction, he was my best friend. That's what was so frustrating. I loved him so much but was unable to help him other than shielding him from the danger he kept putting himself in.

My brother died the way he lived his life--high. I'll never forget the evening I came home and found him dead with a bottle of pills on his table. Maybe this is what made my brother's addiction somewhat more palatable. He wasn't shooting needles into his arms--he was taking prescription pills. My brother wasn't a heroin addict; he was a narcotic addict. Certainly he wouldn't turn a hit of heroin away if he didn't have pills to pop, but pills were his thing. He did "sets." I was soon to learn that terminology after he moved in with me. Sets were combinations of pills that gave you the same high as heroin. Painkillers combined with tranquilizers. Painkillers had the narcotics; the added. The withdrawal was just as potent as a heroin withdrawal. People used to joke that my brother's first stop in their homes was to the bathroom and straight to the medicine cabinet. After a while, people became smarter and hid their pills whenever he would visit, because if they didn't, it was guaranteed that the pills would be gone with him.

One of the reasons why it was difficult for my family to accept that my brother was an addict was because there were no needles that we could visibly see. At first we thought, "He has a problem. It will straighten itself out." He smoked joints of marijuana like they were packs of cigarettes each day. His body was so used to the pot that a dozen joints of them a day just gave him a buzz. It was the narcotics that he needed to get high--and lots of them. If he didn't have his daily dose, he would start to withdraw. And so he went from doctor to doctor, dentist to dentist, pleading for the "scripts" that would take away his pain from withdrawal.

At one point, I convinced him to try methadone so that he wouldn't have to spend his days with scary kinds of people to fix his habit. Bad mistake. He used the methadone to supplement some of his drug needs, but he now had more access to drugs than ever before. The drug dealers were standing outside the drug clinic waiting to sell their wares, and there were lots of anxious buyers--my brother being one of them.

My mother never recovered from the loss of her only son. She also never really talked about him and his addiction. The subject was an understanding of taboo among family members when my mother was around. I know my mother felt that my brother's death was her personal fault because that's the kind of mother she was. She was wonderful and loving. She never did the tough love thing--it was always the unconditional love. She always made excuses for my brother. She aided and abetted his habit to the best of her ability. She felt guilty that she couldn't live with him in the same household because then she had to "face" the fact that he was an addict. As long as he lived 3,000 miles away, it was easy for her to stay in "denial." When my brother moved back here for the last three years of his life, she welcomed him with open arms believing that age had changed him or at least enough love from her would change him. Within a week, she pushed him gently away after having cigarette burns in her couch, bed, and rugs from when he zonked out with butts left in his mouth.

My mother didn't kick my brother out of her place; she just strongly encouraged him to move in with me where there would be more "space." I took him in hoping that we could live without too much conflict. My brother would call my mother several times a week during his more coherent moments, and we tried to keep family gatherings at a minimum during those years knowing that my brother would most likely screw up the holiday. The long-distance relationship of my mother and brother under this short-distance logistical situation kept my mother in better spirits. Maybe that's why it was so hard for her to get past her own unnecessary guilt after my brother died. My mother spent many wasted years after that feeling guilty for something that she had absolutely no control over.

Living with irrational guilt is difficult enough. Living with embarrassing shame makes the situation that much more difficult. I'll never forget the first time months later when someone questioned my mother about the cause of my brother's death at such a young age. She responded, *"He died of heart failure."* I stood there looking at her, but she looked away rather than look at me. I never felt embarrassed about telling people the cause of my brother's death, but my mother never told anyone the real reason. The heart excuse was her stock answer from then on. My mother, who had a difficult time accepting the truth while my brother was alive, had an even more difficult time accepting the truth after he died. But more importantly, she knew the stigma and shame associated with drug addiction. She also knew how society viewed addicts and the parents of addicts. It was so much easier to pretend otherwise.

Because my mother never discussed my brother's addiction, life, or death, even with me, she was never able to find peace within herself. Part of my mother died with my brother and was never able to revive again because it was so buried beneath the guilt and shame. My mother served as a great lesson to me. Unfortunately, this was never a lesson I was planning to learn from. I never knew that I would be walking in my mother's shoes years later with my own daughter and her addiction.

Unlike my mother, I didn't ignore my daughter's addiction and pretend that it would someday go away. I may have been naïve and stupidly optimistic, but I worked her addiction hard. I faced up to it immediately. Although I was divorced from Jennifer's father, we stood as a team throughout her addiction side by side, hand in hand, trying every little trick in the book to get her "unhooked." There was no unhooking her. She was doomed. Heroin was her cancer.

Only a parent who loses a child to this horror can really understand that drug addiction is a disease. Jennifer's father and I always pooh-poohed that terminology whenever we'd talk to the numerous addiction experts that were treating her. To us, the word "disease" was an *excuse* to justify very bad behavior. For every unexplainable bad choice that our daughter made like stealing from both of us, the response was "disease." For every act of bad behavior like rage and cursing, the response was "disease." For every act of irresponsibility like leaving rehab programs and returning to the streets, the response was "disease." Violence? Disease. Dealing? Disease. Prostitution? Disease.

It was only after I went through my various stages of mourning after Jennifer's death that I accepted that her addiction was a disease. At that point, I was able to stop blaming myself for her tragic life and death. And if you think for even one moment that it was the natural course of progression after the death of a child, you are absolutely WRONG. I worked very hard to dissipate those feelings. They just didn't go away on their own. I counseled myself daily using my very best counseling skills. I had to take every irrational feeling of guilt and examine it under a microscope and then let it go. I had to allow myself to drown for a sufficient amount of time before I allowed myself to rescue myself. That's a natural part of mourning after a child dies from drugs.

Now when I think about my daughter and her addiction, I do so with a sense of resolve. My daughter did have a disease--and it was a disease that neither her father nor I were responsible for. We taught our daughter good moral values. She knew the difference between right and wrong. We loved her and nurtured her. We were loving parents who made mistakes because we weren't perfect, but they were the same mistakes all humans make. We tried to save her, but she couldn't save herself.

I have met other wonderful parents of children with drug related deaths. They are loving, kind, caring people who also did their best to stand by their children. None of us raised our children up to be "*irresponsible or foolish.*" *That's what hurts so much, Tad Martin*. In one thoughtless statement, you are judging the 22 years I spent raising my daughter. You negated the moral lessons and values that I taught her every inch of the way. On top of that, you took a very complex problem and with a few trivial words, added to the overpowering shame and self-blame that parents like me swim in day in and day out for years of their lives.

So, next time you have something to say about drugs, Tad, please think about it first. Talk to some parents who have lost their children to the battle of drugs and see how responsible and loving we were. Maybe that way, you'll let people know the truth rather than feed into the distorted stereotypes that society has created around this issue.

This next piece of writing was in my monthly newsletter Straight Talk for women who are married to gay men. In this article, I discuss her homosexuality.

IN MEMORY OF MY DAUGHTER JENNIFER

My daughter, Jennifer, age 22, died on April 14, 2002. Her young life was snuffed out due to medical complications from a serious drug addiction to heroin that overtook her life starting three-and-a-half years ago.

I would like to thank the dozens of people who were alerted through the various Straight Spouse groups who sent me beautiful messages of warmth and comfort. Your words have been overwhelmingly supportive and kind. The members of my own on-line support group have been extremely generous in their love and support. I would like to take a few moments to share some personal thoughts about the relationship between my daughter and me in hopes that it will shed some insight to those of you who are part of this large network.

As I reflect on the years that I had my daughter, I can say with good feelings that I take comfort knowing that I did everything humanly possible to help her through her troubled years. When I first learned of her addiction two months before the age of 19, I immediately admitted her into a drug recovery program, the first of a dozen or so that she entered and dropped from until her death. It was during this first stint that I learned that Jennifer was a lesbian. She did not reveal this information to me. Rather I found out from some of her friends when she ran away from the program with another young lady during her second month there. When she came to visit me several days later, I asked her why she never told me about her sexuality. I felt hurt that I had to find it out from her friends because she didn't trust me enough to tell me. When she responded that she was afraid of hurting me, I was very confused and asked her why.

I had raised my daughter to be understanding and tolerant of homosexuality. From the time she was a young child, I was very careful to project positive images of gay people. I developed some wonderful gay friends through my support group in the 1980's who were part of her life. I was very emphatic in telling her that gay people had no choice in their homosexuality--they were born that way. I felt the need to reinforce that regularly for two reasons. First, I never wanted her to feel that her father "chose" homosexuality over his family. It was difficult enough living in a homophobic world without thinking that a father would prefer that way of life if given a choice. But more importantly, I knew statistically that children with a gay parent had a higher chance of being gay themselves. My years of research had proven that to me. I believe that gay is genetic, and it would only follow that the gene could be passed on to some of the children. I was always able to separate my anger towards my ex-husband's irresponsibility from homosexuality.

My daughter's response: "Mom, I didn't want to hurt you because I know how much dad has put you through." I was stumped. I asked her if I ever led her to believe that I had a problem with homosexuality. She said, "Absolutely not." I next asked her if she thought I would be disappointed that she was a lesbian. She replied, "I'm not sure." No matter how accepting I felt about homosexuality, and no matter how many times I said it would never bother me if my children were gay, she wasn't sure when it became a reality if I would feel the same way.

Truthfully, I was initially numb when I found out that Jennifer was a lesbian. Was I happy about it? No. But it wasn't because of homosexuality. I just knew how much harder life would be for her as a gay person. But, after the initial numbness passed in a day or two, I fell into an easy acceptance. Homosexuality was never an issue for me when it came to my daughter. Her drug problem was my only concern. I embraced all of her girlfriends over the next three years hoping she would find one that would give her a greater sense of stability and happiness.

Some people have asked me if I thought my daughter's drug habit resulted from her homosexuality. After all, drugs and alcohol are a common problem in the gay community. That's because the pain of being gay is too difficult for many who don't have accepting mothers. This was not Jennifer's case. She had no problem being a lesbian. That was one area of her life that she was totally comfortable and happy about. She had a large "PRIDE" tattoo engraved on her arm several years ago with all of the rainbow colors. She became active in the gay recovery movement during the times when she was clean. In fact, last year when she had her longest clean period of six months, she worked at the drug recovery booth at the Philadelphia Gay Pride parade. She laughed at the end of the day when she brought me a bunch of leftover flavored condoms she gave out at the booth saying, "Ma, you need these more than I do."

When I think back to the day I revealed my daughter's homosexuality to my ex-husband shortly after I first learned about it, I remember the great irony of that moment. He went on a screaming rampage that shocked even me. He started yelling, "How could she do this?" He then went on to blurt out a number of obscenities. I was really stumped. He was sure that it the drugs were turning her "temporarily" gay. Over the next few years, he came up with numerous theories about Jennifer's homosexuality and tried to convince her that it was just a "passing phase" that would change if she overcame her addiction. He was embarrassed by Jennifer's comfort with her sexuality because he was so uncomfortable with his own homosexuality. When she would visit him and he had company, he would ask her to cover the tattoo. He constantly bemoaned the fact that now she wouldn't have grandchildren, and periodically kept hoping that she would at least meet a man and have a grandchild to carry on his legacy. What can I say?

The funniest thing is he would occasionally try to blame me for Jennifer's homosexuality stating that I must have been too much of an "overbearing mother," similar to the one he had. My ex just didn't buy into the genetic inborn thing when it concerned him. He made sure to tell me on various occasions, "Don't try to blame me. It has nothing to do with me. After all, I wasn't born gay." He always feels better thinking that he was "made" gay and not born that way. I never blamed him, I just stated my feelings that it was a passed on gene. Homosexuality is not a "fault" to be blamed on anyone. People have no control over this anymore than they have control over their eye color.

When my ex wasn't blaming the drugs, he would blame her appearance. Jennifer was a heavy-set young woman and he believed her lack of an attractive figure made her believe that she had more options finding women than men. This was his craziness in thinking. In my heart, I believe that he feared people would question *his* carefully hidden sexuality if they knew she was gay. As usual, it was always about him. And yet, in some of his more vulnerable moments, he would admit that he was glad that she was comfortable with her sexuality, even if he wasn't comfortable with his.

Last July, my daughter fell in love with a woman. They were both in programs at that point and met through the recovery community. There is a rule in the recovery world that states people should avoid romantic relationships until they are clean for at least a year. This is based on statistics that show people who get romantically involved with other people in recovery during the first year are likely to relapse together under pressure. Go tell that to a young woman whose hormones are raging and need to feel love and security are at their height. Jennifer knew the rule but couldn't abide by it. She had a string of involvements over the past few years, but none that lasted for any length of time until she met Raina. Raina had been clean for eleven months. It didn't take long for them to fall down together shortly after they met. I accepted this woman as if she were my own daughter, even though her own family had abandoned her. She took care of Jennifer the best that she could. They were totally intertwined in their love and their addiction. They would try to pull each other up, and then they would knock each other down.

I certainly don't blame Raina for my daughter's demise. Jennifer did that all on her own. She developed hepatitis and a bowel instruction brought on by the heroin. This was also complicated by chronic asthma. In the end, her drug-ravaged body just gave out.

There is a point I would like to make in sharing this story with you. Over the past two weeks since this tragedy, I have been processing a lot of emotional feelings, which is natural under the circumstances. When my moments of rationale surpass my emotionalism, I sit down and add to this tribute because my thoughts are clearer. I think one of the best gifts I gave my daughter throughout her life was unconditional love regardless of who she was or what she did. I also feel a great sense of relief that my daughter didn't have to struggle with one additional problem in her short-lived life, namely her sexuality. I never made her hide her tattoo or gave her any indication that I loved her any less or differently because she was a lesbian. She was very appreciative and stated that to me during numerous conversations between the two of us and with her friends. I embraced her girlfriends and never made them feel like I judged them because I did not. I was proud that my daughter felt comfortable in who she was, at least sexually. Being gay did not turn her into a drug addict. As I said earlier, I was always able to separate my anger of what my ex-husband did to me during and after our marriage from my feelings about homosexuality. Because I could do this, I have hundreds of wonderful memories to carry with me through the empty years ahead.

There is something you can learn from my experience and tragedy. Homosexuality is not a choice. Don't transfer your personal anger against your gay husband to your children in terms of the sexuality issue. You don't know how the sexuality of your children will end up. If they sense your hostility towards homosexuality, it may create years of hardship for them to come to terms with themselves, just like it happened to your husband. It can also alienate you from having a loving relationship with your children.

I know I've passed this message on before, but now, more than ever, it needs to be said again.

++++++++++++++++++++++++++++++

For all of the mothers who are reading this, please love your children and don't let sexuality be the issue. Life is so precious and fragile. Love your children for who they are and not for what they are. Because I was able to accept Jennifer's homosexuality, I will have my wonderful memories to hang on to through the years even though I no longer have her. And I will always feel proud that I was the kind of mother that Jennifer was proud to have.

Rest in peace my beautiful baby. Your mother will always love you.

CHAPTER SIX

JENNIFER'S WORDS

Jennifer left behind some impactful writing. I hope that others who are going through her struggle or contemplating it will listen to her words and make better choices. Some of these are letters she wrote to me; others are poems she wrote. Some are very raw expressing how she felt. I have left the writing in its original form without correcting it.

If you have a child whom you believe is involved with drugs, please share Jennifer's poems with him or her. Maybe seeing the suffering she was going through will help your child. Many years ago when Jennifer started writing her poems, she told me to share them with anyone who might be able to get help from them.

March 21, 1999
Mom,

I'm sorry it's taken me so long to write you a letter, but my mind has been really cloudy.

It's hard for me to express what I'm feeling in a letter. I guess I'm feeling scared, lonely, depressed, etc. Mom, I'm really sorry for the pain I put you through. I never meant to hurt anybody. I didn't even mean to hurt myself. It's just that dope took me by the ass and kicked me. I never intended on being an addict. It just happened. I couldn't stop. Nothing else mattered to me. I just didn't want to feel the pain. Not only the physical pain, but the mental pain of my life. I couldn't cope with life on life's terms. So drugs blocked out all of the mental shit. I've had a really hard time dealing with life with dad being gay and abusive mentally. I've had a hard time trying to communicate with you. I've had a hard time thinking about my little brother being sick. I've had the hardest time dealing with myself. I don't really know what my problem is. I don't know why I love violence, crime, drugs and that lifestyle. I've always loved beating someone up and watching them suffer. I do feel remorse, but not until the damage is already done. That's why I loved gangs and all of that dumb shit. Mom, I've hurt so many innocent people in and out of my addiction. I can barely live with myself. I ask for God's forgiveness every night but I don't think I'm ready to forgive myself. I pray one day you will be able to forgive me for the pain I put you through. I know seeing your own daughter go through what your brother went through kills you. I don't ever want you to think for a second that this was your fault. I did this to myself. You were and are the greatest mother in the world. I never felt unloved or unprovided for. I know you sacrificed to give to me. And I love you for it. Mom, I'm trying real hard to change my ways. Not only my lifestyle, but my attitude towards everything. I want to be a better person. It's just so hard to cope without drugs. I can't stop thinking about getting high. I obsess over it. I hope it starts to get easier. I hope I can learn to live without drugs but I don't know if I can. I promise you mom I'm going to try damn hard to.

I love you very much. Thank you for all your love and support. Without it I would be back on drugs.

Love ya
Jennifer

(no date)
Mom,

Well today you drove me home from Friends (*Hospital for psychiatric problems*). You asked me to write you so that's what I'm doing. Mom you do so much for me, like today how you bought me so much. I feel bad because I know you can't afford it. It makes me feel like such a piece of shit taking it from you. I should have my life together and be supporting myself. But look at me, I'm at square 1 all over again. I can't express to you enough how grateful I am for you. It breaks my heart to see you cry because of me and my stupidity. I know this much, I'm tired and fed up. I never want to go through this shit again. Most of all, I don't want to drag you through my shit with me. When I get high, I never think of what it's doing to you. I'm so sorry for everything. Mom, I'm really trying to change. I don't expect you to believe me or trust me. But I know over time I will earn your trust back. I really hate living here but I'm not complaining because I know I put myself here. I've been writing poetry, I don't know why, but I know I express myself better on paper. It's like I have so much to say, but my mind is racing and it comes out better on paper. Remember how you used to tell me I was quick witted and should be a lawyer. Well, I guess drugs fucked up my wit. I never can express in words how I feel because my mind's always racing. I notice in arguments I don't have fast comebacks like I used to. Maybe it's because I feel the after effect drugs have had on my mind. Maybe my mind will regroup after this is over. I hope so. Well that's about all I got to say except I love you very much more than you will ever know.

XOXOXOXOXOXOX
Love,
Jen

(no date)
Mom,

Hi mom. How ya doing. I'm ok today. I'm fed up with this rehab, but I know I don't have a choice. I miss you and Jason. This all feels like a nightmare that I can't wake up from. It's so hard for me to accept the fact that I relapsed. So anyway I wrote these 3 poems. I never wrote poems before so I figured maybe I can express how I feel. When I am better with some time I'll look at them to remind me how I felt.

Love ya
Jen

October 28, 1999
7 days clean and miserable

I sit and wonder why I always have to go back to
getting high
I wish being normal was automatic but I have
accepted I'm nothing but an addict
Sometimes I sit for hours and cry beggin' God just to
tell me why
I prey at night to be released from this hell
Will it get any better, I can't really tell
I hate myself for things I've done
I remember a time when life was fun
Now my body is beggin' me for dope
I feel so lost without any hope
If I was high now I would feel no pain
But slowly I'm going insane
I know I have to do this on my own
But never in my life have I felt so alone
It's so hard for me to go on and persist
I'm starting to think it would be easier to slice my wrist
At least in death I will find peace
It has to be better than the street

October 29, 1999
8 days clean

Walking up and down the Ave.
desperation was all I had
No money in my pocket and feeling sick
I need that bag even if I have to suck a dick
I'm beggin' my addiction to just subside,
give me happiness and a little pride
Why did I relapse. I'm so dumb.
My brain and body are so fuckin' numb
Self esteem I've never had none
I can't remember the last time I had fun
There is something I must admit
For all the wrong I've done I deserve this shit
I can't live like this much longer
Because my addiction is growing stronger
All I'm asking for is my life back
But my desire is always going to attack
It plays on me and knows I'm weak
It says the drugs I have to seek
It's almost as my life isn't real
I wish somebody knew exactly how I feel

November 1, 1999
11 days clean

I'm sitting here trying to cope
I'm trying to live life without a bag of dope
I'm starting to feel good and a little strong
But my addictions telling me it won't be long
My bag of dope was my only friend
I thought it would be with me till the very end
The hurt I've caused to my father, brother, and mother
Especially to me that's why I have to recover

This is a piece that Jennifer wrote in 1999. I couldn't read it until recently. I had already titled this book "Jennifer Needle in Her Arm." Sure enough, I see now it was the right title to get her point across to those reading this.

November 5, 1999

I'm in such a state of confusion.
I can't figure out what I want.
To die with a needle in my arm.
Can I find serenity within that?
To stay sober and miserable I just can't do it.
I don't want to feel pain. I don't want stress. I want sedation.
I don't even want to know what's going on in the world around me.
Can't I just be numb?
I'm 19 but feel 59.
I'm not worried about death because I'm living in hell.
I wish somebody could understand me!
I wish I could erase the past.
I hate living in today.
I want to live in a better tomorrow.

November 6, 1999

I can't sleep, but I don't want to stay awake.
The urge to use has taken me over once again.
My addiction is calling.
But I won't answer.
I won't answer because it tells me what I want to hear.
How could I let anything destroy me like heroin has?
It's taken so much from me.
But worse of it's taken me from me.
It knows what I want.
It plays off my weakness.
It sneaks up on me when I least expect it.
When my disease strikes it takes everything in its path.
It's so fuckin' powerful.
But I'll never stop fighting, until it kills me.

November 7, 1999

I wish I could go to sleep and wake up in a year.
Just think 1 year sober, parent's trust, car, job, school.
I see these things but yet they're too far to grab.
Can I live in a half normal life?
Is being sober a punishment, because it sure feels
like one.
I'm sick and tired of being sick and tired.
I don't want to use to live and live to use.
I just want to live.
Why is that such a hard obstacle?

November 8, 1999

Tired of the same old shit.
Same old game.
Same old results.
How many times do I need to fuck up, to come to the realization that drugs can't be a part of my life?
Tired of living for nothing.
Tired of nothing coming from living.
Does anybody feel like I do?
Desperation has taken over my emotions.
I want to cry but just can't.
Tired of making up lies.
My whole life is one big huge LIE!!!!

November 10, 1999

As anger rushes through my body it reminds me of the rush from a needle. The only thing that's different is I can feel. Anger doesn't make the hurt go away. I wish I felt numb. I want to want recovery. I just don't have the desire. I wish I knew where to find the desire. Was this my last run?

Please God let it be!!

November 12, 1999

Walking up and down the avenue trying to figure out
what to do.
The sickness is coming.
I can feel it in my stomach.
Cars are pulling over asking if I am working or just
asking how much?
I keep walking.
I've already done that shit and I don't feel that low.
But as time goes on the sickness grows stronger.
Now I'm waiting for someone to pull over.
When I get in the car all I keep thinking is why me?
When I'm done and I cop my dope, I forget about
what I just had to do.
In fact I forget about everything.

November 13, 1999

I wonder if my life will ever change.
Then again I fear change.
I don't know how to live when I'm not chemically intoxicated.
I've been to hell and back.
I wonder when it will be my turn to see heaven.
Will God forgive me for desecrating myself and so many others?
I hope so.
I've wanted to die so many times and just didn't have the heart to do it.
Maybe there's a purpose for me to live behind all this insanity.

November 18, 1999
28 days clean

There's a tale of a twisted fate
With pain and horror you cannot contemplate
Life is unbearable it's plain to see
Seems like nothing can kill what's inside of me
Loneliness and hurt I everyday feel
Knowing that not even God could heal
With one prick from a needle to my skin
I hear some yell "LET THE NUMBNESS BEGIN"
It's a rush going through my body as a whole
But it moves fast and eats away at my soul
This is my life, but I will never win
Because of it I've committed sin after sin
I never gain power or any control
I choose this life rather than to be dull
I want to be normal and enjoy being young
I feel my head in a rope ready to be hung
I beg and prey for a fucking cure
How much agony can one girl endure
Is this God's way of showing spite
At the end of the tunnel I see no light
It makes me not want to put up a fight
And I feel like this night after night

December 6, 1999
Mom,

I hope you had a nice vacation in New York. (*I spent Thanksgiving with my mother who was dying from cancer*) I was really obsessing on getting out of here. Not to get high, just to get away from all this petty shit. But I figured I got myself in here, so I have to deal with it. I really do miss you mom. I've been thinking a lot, and think we should both take one night a week and spend some quality time together. I sure hope you don't take any blame for me being a screw up. I did this to myself. You were a great mother, and I manipulated you and took advantage of your kindness. I'm so sorry mom. I pray to god every night that you will someday forgive me and even one day trust me. It's so hard for me to understand why I keep doing this to myself. I just don't know why. I'll never give up this battle though. I can't make you anymore fake promises about my sobriety. I can just promise you I will not give up, and I'll never give in to this addiction no matter how many times I screw up. I hope this is the last time. I can't deal with this disease anymore.

Read my letter to my addiction

Love,
Jen

Dear addiction,

What have I ever done to you to deserve all this pain and agony? You have taken everything from me. My family's trust, my family's sleep, my sleep, my apartment, car, jewelry, etc. But worst of all you've taken my sanity, my life, and me. I think of you every day. I even dream about you at night. I'm sure your only thoughts about me are to totally destroy me. I love you yet hate you so much. No matter how hard I fight you are stronger. I'm 19 but feel 69 because of you. You have robbed me of my childhood. Because of you I have killed, robbed, sold drugs, sold myself, and hurt everyone close to me. You're a liar!!!! You swore you would make things easier for me. You swore I wouldn't have to worry about anything. You promised fun and heaven. But all you have given me is hurt and agony and a living hell. This is my life and I'm taking it back. I'm going to win this battle.

I PROMISE

February 19, 2000
Dear Mom,

Well I don't really have much to write. I just got done at welfare and everything was fine. I have 13 days clean. I still feel like shit because I lost my 6 months. But somebody told me not to look at it this way. He said I still have 6 months of recovery. Knowledge and tools. I guess that's a more positive way to look at it. I really do miss you mom. I swear things will be better for me and you. I'm starting to get honest with myself, about myself. I'm also talking a lot in counseling. I know my life will get better than this.

Well talk to ya later

Love,
Jen

May 17, 2001
Mom,

How are you? I'm ok, but feel kind of weird being here. It's hard to follow all of these rules, but I'm willing to do what it takes to be sober. I realized how bad I screwed up. The only thing I can do is keep trying. I have no desire to get high. The only thing is I have to learn to cope with everything without getting high. I guess it's easier said than done. I really do appreciate all of your help and support through everything. I really want to do the right thing this time. I know you feel powerless regarding me getting high but I'm the powerless one. But with all your support it sure does help me stay sober, and want it all more. I don't know where I would be without you mom. I promise one day I'll repay you. You deserve a lot better than what I have become. I know I will be better one day. Well I can't use the phone for 10 days, and I can't get visitors for 2 weeks. So I guess we can be pen pals for a while.

Love,
Jen

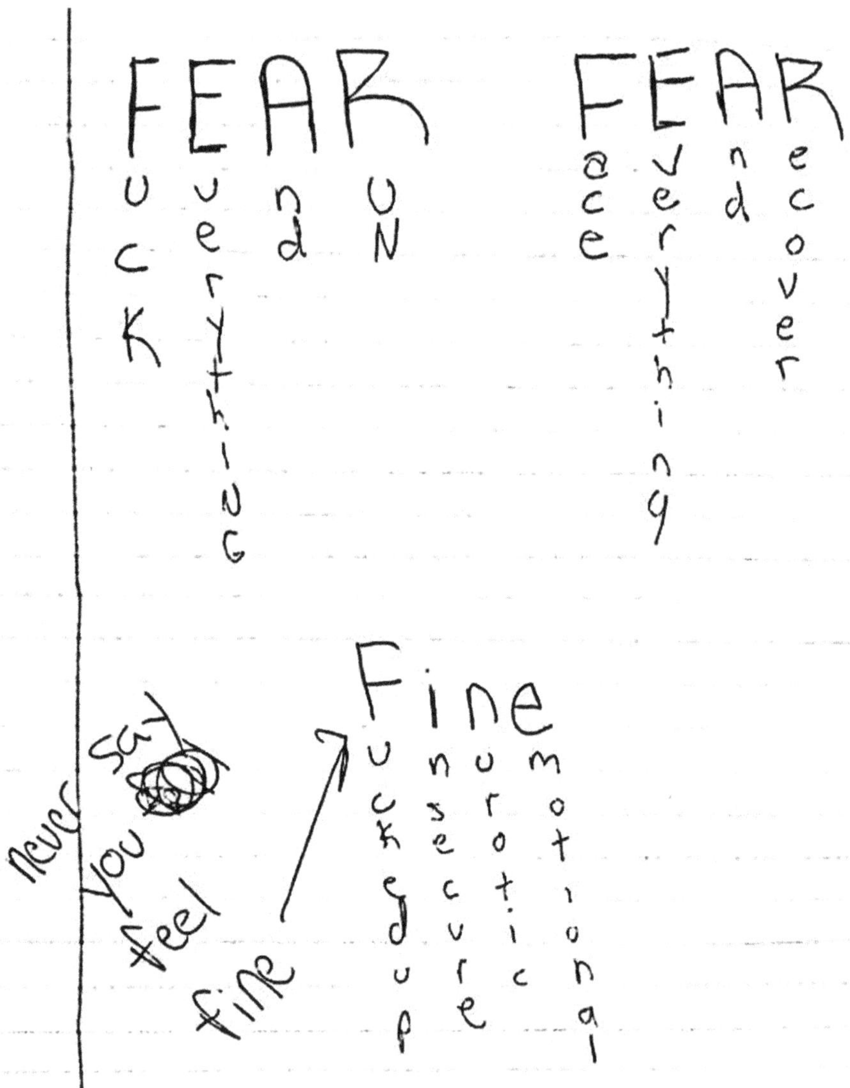
FEAR
uck
verything
nd
UN
FEAR
ace
verything
nd
ecover
never say you feel fine
Fine
ucked up
nsecure
eurotic
motional

<u>CONCLUSION</u>

The message that I hope that Jennifer and I conveyed to you is that this is not the life that either of us thought would ever happen. A lot of this was beyond both of us. I try not to look back and re-dig up all of the old hurt. It serves no purpose. I have seen other parents do very detrimental things to themselves following the death of their children.

It would be easy for me to fall into a very dark hole after the loss of both of my children. I could easily dig myself in there and never come back. But I haven't done that. Why? Because I believe in purpose. I have a purpose--and my work on earth isn't done yet. There are still people who need help, and it is my job to reach out and help them.

If you feel that this book has helped you, then I have accomplished my goal. I am happy to give you support as you go through your own grieving whether your child has died or is in the process of killing himself/herself. All you have to do is reach out, and I will be there for you.

Write to me at **Bonkaye@aol.com**. You can also contact me through my personal page on Facebook at:

https://www.facebook.com/pages/Bonnie-Kaye-Author/759401654100143

Jennifer Needle in Her Arm

ABOUT THE AUTHOR

Bonnie Kaye is an internationally recognized relationship counselor/author. She is also an educator working with adult high school dropouts to obtain their high school equivalency diploma. She is the director of the Northeast GED Center in Philadelphia, Pennsylvania. Kaye also has a book co-op for independent authors at:

www.BooksofExcellence.com

She also has an Internet radio show on Sunday evenings for those authors.

In 2002, Kaye lost her daughter, Jennifer, at the age of 22 to a three-and-a-half-year heroin addiction. Afterwards, she started a local weekly support group for other parents who were suffering with this catastrophe to help them in the healing process. She stopped the group after nearly a year, unable to do her own healing. Instead, she has done personal one-on-one counseling with parents who requested her help over the past decade.

Kaye's other books include: *The Gay Husband Checklist for Women Who Wonder; Straight Wives: Shattered Lives (Volumes 1 and 2); ManReaders: A Woman's Guide to Dysfunctional Men; Bonnie Kaye's Straight Talk; How I Made My Husband Gay: Myths About Straight Wives; Doomed Grooms: Gay and Bisexual Husbands in Straight Marriages; Gay Husbands Say the Darndest Things* and *Over the Cliff: Gay Husbands in Straight Marriages.*

www.ingramcontent.com/pod-product-compliance
Lightning Source LLC
Chambersburg PA
CBHW021337090426
42742CB00008B/634

* 9 7 8 1 7 7 1 4 3 1 6 1 3 *